Empower

Publishing

Also by Louse Gore Sayer David

John Steel: The Man and the Legend

The She Heard a Whippoorwill Cry Series:
Green Sea Plantation
The Land Darkens
Spring's Gift of Light
The Turbulence and the Storm
The Winds Grow Gentle
The Gathering

The Religious Awakening of Sirus Smith

To Shatter a Cherished Possession

and *Empower Publishing*

Half Harvest

Book Seven in the She Heard a
Whippoorwill Series

By

Louise Gore Sayre-David

Empower Publishing
Winston-Salem

Empower

Publishing

Empower Publishing
PO Box 26701
Winston-Salem, NC 27114

First Empower Publishing Books edition published January, 2024
Empower Publishing, Feather Pen, and all production design are trademarks.

For information regarding bulk purchases of this book, digital purchase and special discounts, please contact the publisher at publish.empower.now@gmail.com

Cover design by Pan Morrelli

Manufactured in the United States of America
ISBN 978-1-63066-590-6

In loving memory of my parents, Webb and Dora Gore, and siblings.

Mary Doratheta
Daniel Lucian
Joseph Thurman
Clayton Luke
Hubert Rudolph
Carrie Emma
Sally Edna
Lacy Leadonis

—Louise Gore Sayre-David

Chapter One

In the years that were to ensue that October Sunday of 1887, fortune was to smile on Eliza Heyward, breathing a blessedness into each waking day that was to fill her with untold love and joy. Indeed, Eliza came to look back on this span of time in her life – from this momentous Sunday of 1887 to the year 1890 – as being the most rewarding in the way of personal happiness that she was to ever experience. Yes, halcyon years, for Eliza they were until that sixth sense of hers began to forewarn her that this golden period was marked, which, of course, brought a deep untimely sadness raining down on her even before this peaceful period was to end.

However, as Eliza looked back on this period of time in later years and reflected over it, she also came to feel that she had made it count to the fullest, telling herself that if it had run into a whole decade instead of the three short years that it did last that she could not have crammed anymore happiness into those ten years than she had crammed into those three. For that Sunday celebration with family and friends was only the beginning, the beginning of that new course that Eliza had reasoned she should follow, a course that she had found was so rewarding and satisfying that she literally mourned the thought of it veering one degree from its present set form. At times, since the move that she had decided upon that October Sunday had obviously been so well-timed, Eliza found herself wondering if that intense second sight of hers had made her aware all along that that was the day she should resume her churchgoing! Not that it mattered that much to her anymore due to the way things had turned out! Still, the thought did persist in crossing her mind from time to time.

At any rate, the restoration of family unity had and was giving Eliza great satisfaction. In fact, she made this clear to everybody by the frequency in which she had family members

1

as well as close friends seated around the huge dining table at Green Sea helping her partake of still another celebration of some kind. All the same, these intimate gatherings with family and friends were by no means the whole of Eliza's resumed social doings. For if she was not celebrating some family member's birthday or wedding anniversary with a dinner party at Green Sea, to say nothing of her afternoon teas or numerous quilting bees she staged, she was dashing off to attend someone else's quilting bee or social get-together. In addition, there were the more gala affairs as well, the corn huskings and the barn raisings, the barn dances and dinner dances and the more formal balls, all of which of course, were ever more exciting to Eliza. For not only did these social affairs call for the attendance of both sexes, but – often as not – saw the whole family attending as well, children along with grownups. To be more direct in point of Eliza's social life, nowadays if she was not staging the entertainment herself at Green Sea, one could bet she was being entertained someplace else!

Eliza's relationship with Stuart Drakston was pleasant enough. The fact was, if Stuart jangled Eliza's nerves every now and then, or made her feel her newfound serenity was drawing to a close, it was not because of their past differences or anything relating to or bearing on their past quarrels. It was due to what Eliza felt was Stuart's over-eagerness to hover over the twins – Jane Anne too for that matter – and keep them within his sight constantly. Forcing herself to be mild about it she had attempted on several occasions to make Stuart see that all children needed to run free and explore a little, telling him that besides the educational element involved that the freedom of seeking and choosing their own entertainment without his say would give the twins self-confidence. Seeing, however, that any amount of advice or opinions that she had given or was ready to offer on the subject of child rearing was not changing Stuart's over-worry attitude at all, she finally decided that before they began to lock horns over it that the best thing for her to do was to let the matter drop. Of course, thanks to the exuberant presence of Matt Heyward, Eliza's other adored grandchild, her decision to have any more say on the subject had not been hard for her to make! For Eliza was certain where she had failed in gaining some freedom for the twins that Matt was going to succeed; in that, he did explore and explored plenty and the twins were of a mind to accompany him despite their father's fret or his disapproval. And, in addition, there was also the matter of Stuart trying to keep pace with the children every time that he and Jane Ann came to Green Sea. To Eliza's way of thinking most grownups soon grew weary of chasing after children and Stuart was going to be no exception to that rule!

Yes, Matt Heyward and his father and mother were all permanent residents of Green Sea now, having moved from Lexington, Virginia, some months earlier when Carr Heyward had finally completed his major in law at the University of Virginia. Like Stuart Drakston before him, Carr had come back home and set up his law office, choosing to practice his profession in Green Sea's healthful atmosphere instead of the polluted air and noise in Charleston. And Carr's law business was flourishing. In fact, he was now the factor of a number of Stuart's clients simply because Stuart was finding it more and more difficult to meet the demands his law practice required and see to the management of Drakston Hall's vast acreage too – a responsibility that had recently become his since the aged and frail Matthew Carson could handle it no longer. Carr Heyward was not only seeing to the legal matters of his own clients and those of whom he had gained through Stuart, but he was also helping Stuart out when the latter found himself falling behind in the duties of his law work. Actually, what it all measured up to and even though they did maintain separate offices, Stuart and Carr had become law partners. But, even so, they conducted not one fraction of legal business for Luke Heyward! Holding fast to his moral makeup, Luke continued to take all business of legal matters to Bill Cooper, something he had done from the day that Bill Cooper had also become a practicing attorney. Still, both Stuart and Carr were not surprised and understood because they were no stranger to the way of Luke Heyward's nature.

Yes, the mansion at Green Sea pulsed in lively rhythm nowadays. For besides five grownups living under its roof once again there was the heir to Green Sea living there now as well – the dynamic three-year-old Matt whose appealing deep violet eyes and dark brown curls made him almost exempt from the sting of the switch no matter what kind of mischief he pulled. Of course, all three grandchildren had come to be very dear and precious to Eliza and Luke. In fact, Matt and the Drakston twins, Frankie and Lizzie, were filling Eliza's and Luke's days with such joy that not one day ended that they did not feel as though they had regaled in some exciting adventure of some kind. And, often as not, that was precisely what had taken place and especially since Matt had come to live at Green Sea. For Matt's exuberant presence hardly left one idle moment for any of the grownups he dwelled with. Indeed, about the only time that Matt came to a standstill, so to speak, from the time he rose from his bed in the morning till he fell back into it at night, was at mealtime or when he found himself sitting between Eliza and Luke in the buggy headed for Drakston Hall to visit with the twins, and these visits were a sure thing to take place if as many as two days passed without Frankie and Lizzie showing up at Green Sea.

Although she never voiced her dislike for the name, Eliza Heyward did not go for the girl twin being called Lizzie. Eliza thought the name sounded too flat and unadorned for the little girl, whose blond flowing curls and demure mien could not have made her appear more feminine and doll-like. Indeed, she refused to call the girl twin Lizzie unless the situation forced her to, preferring to call her only granddaughter, her curled darling, or even Pullet sometimes, which, of course, did decry the little girl's femininity far more than if she had gone ahead and addressed the little girl as Lizzie! But Eliza's opinion continued to hold, because she thought most any name would have been far more suitable for the little girl than Lizzie! Eliza had no idea who had come up with the name of Lizzie. But she suspected it was Stuart Drakston since he had decided that she herself had spoken the truth that long ago October day when she had said the twin girl was the very image of Elizabeth Drakston!

Eliza still clung to the notion that the name Frankie was appropriate enough for the boy twin's name. If the name affected her to any degree when she addressed him as Frankie, it was a deep regret that Frank Drakston was not there to look upon the chubby little fellow and take delight in his presence too.

Taking all three grandchildren on an outing got to be a commonplace thing to do with Eliza and Luke in this third summer of the children's young lives. Quite often, and most the time, Phil Carson came along too, they took Matt, Frankie and Lizzie on picnics and also took them to Charleston on shopping sprees. They waded with them in the shallow parts of the river and, eventually, taught all three children to swim. They went fishing a lot too, but more for the sport and fun of going with the children than thinking that the trip was going to pay off with a few bream or perch to fry for supper, because holding any notion that three energetic children were going to stay quiet and not scare the fish away was too absurd to hope for.

At any rate, there were other activities to engage in too. For example, teaching the children to stay on the backs of their ponies without falling off and taking them to O'Henry's General Store for their usual treat – a small brown paper bag of mouthwatering candy for each child. Indeed, it gave Eliza and Luke both a lot of pleasure to obseve the children as each one made their own candy selection from the huge mounds of candy that O'Henry kept in a glass showcase. And, no question, the children themselves never failed to marvel over the fact that the proprietor, who was quite elderly by this time, would exchange a whole bag of his delectable candy for the one buffalo nickel, or sometimes the five pennies, that they let drop in his hand.

Yes, not only had Eliza Heyward reshaped most of her

views and set herself on an entirely different course and all for the love of family at that, but these joyful experiences with her grandchildren were making this the most laughter-loving summer of her whole life – in fact so merry and good that time and again she felt as though she were dancing the summer away!

Certainly, the whole of Eliza's thoughts as well as her range of vision could not have been clearer and unladen with worry. Even on dark, cloud-capped days the sky seemed sunny to her with not one blemish marring the distant horizon. No gloom, no fore-feeling whatever that one shadow was going to darken her pathway. As a matter of fact, the one little fret that she had acknowledged and given thought to, which was how well she and the strong-willed Beth Anne were going to hit it off now that they were living under the same roof had all been for naught. For there was nothing but harmony between them. No rivalry for Carr's or young Matthew's devotion. Nor any conflict over who was first lady of the household either!

Of course, from that day long back when Beth Anne had gotten her first glimpse of Green Sea, she had been keenly attracted to it and all the things its properties represented – a legacy passing from one generation to another. And, giving thought to all those bygone lifetimes and the legacies passed down through those years – those men and women, too, whom had made it all possible and brought Green Sea to what it had become affected Beth Anne so profoundly that it brought her to feel that in some way and somehow there was a tie between her and all her eyes were taking in! And, as strange as it was, the feeling that she was tied in some mysterious way to the vast fortune she was taking in had nothing at all to do with Carr Heyward her fiancée and present heir to Green Sea. Then later with the true identity of her father coming to light, she began to understand why she felt so emotionally tied to Green Sea from the beginning. So, feeling attached to it from the start it was not too difficult for her to exchange the devotion she held for her home in Lexington and leave the latter and come to Green Sea and call it home. In addition, besides the heritage that awaited her in South Carolina and all the importance she attached to it, knowing the house that she had grown up in in Lexington was not going to echo with the footfalls of strangers when she had walked out of it had had a great deal to do with how well Beth Anne had adjusted to the set customs and rules that had ever been practiced in the mansion at Green Sea. For no sooner than Beth Anne, her father and Carr had moved out of the house that Philippe Carson had so painstakingly built for his late wife, Rachelle, Gilford Sloan and his bride Lucy Randolph had moved into it. Yes, aware that her uncle Gilford had purchased the house and small estate from her father and he and his bride would occupy it had made her move to the Carolina Lowcountry a lot easier for Beth Anne than had it been otherwise.

At any rate, once Phillippe Carson's daughter was settled into the mansion at Green Sea, she seemed to fit into its pattern of everyday living like an old worn glove, appearing to be – and indeed she was – more than happy to let the household routine stay as it was and change nothing about it even if it did mean playing a less dominant role than she was used to when it came to the matter of home-making. The fact was, Beth Anne was far more interested in what went on in Carr's law office and helping him out with some of his law duties like filing his papers and helping with his correspondence than she was in making out daily menus and seeing to all the other duties that fell to the mistress of a household anyhow. So, playing second fiddle to Eliza Heyward in that respect suited Beth Anne just fine! And, what's more, it suited Carr Heyward too. He enjoyed having Beth Anne at his side as much as she enjoyed being there. Still very much enamored with one another, their hours together never seemed long enough. Indeed, the hours they spent in Carr's law office seemed no different and as much enjoyable to them as their nonworking hours. Still, for all their treasured time together, the one thing that took priority over everything else and led the blissful dance in their marriage was their son, Matt. They both adored him. But, even so, and as much as Matt was their pride and joy, they did not mind sharing him with others, namely his doting grandparents, all three of them!

Certainly, life was good and had come to be a happy time for Eliza Heyward and her family, a delightful year until the summer days began to wane into an early autumn and then, for Eliza, her days became haunted by that old familiar uneasiness all over again. It fell in the way of her every step, dogging her every move and her every turn so closely that on one cold, gray day in November when she found herself sitting beside Matthew Carson's deathbed – observing his labored breathing – she was not surprised in the least to find herself there. Indeed, even before Eliza had gone ahead and joined the other family members at the breakfast table that morning, she had known that Doctor Seth Roalf's message that had come before breakfast was over with was on its way to her. Seth Roalf had wasted no words regarding the seriousness of his patient's condition. Instead of going into a lot of professional humbug about the fainting spell that Matthew Carson had suffered early that morning, the doctor had come straight out and said in his message that he did not expect Eliza's father to live out the day! Of course, Eliza and all the other family members living at Green Sea had made ready to leave for Drakston Hall immediately.

And now, with one and all having paid his or her short, solemn respects to the obviously fading Matthew Carson and leaving Eliza behind to sit with him a spell as he had requested, Eliza, tearful and heavy hearted, had pulled a straight chair up closer beside the bed and falling into it she began to wait, waiting for her father to tell her what was on his mind, if anything.

Finally, after some few minutes, minutes in which Eliza had not dared to take her fixed gaze from her father's closed, glasslike eyelids, Matthew Carson suddenly letting his eyelids lift and mastering a strength that almost made Eliza feel as though her fears and premonitions were going to turn out to be a deception after all, said, "Don't darling girl, don't grieve for me. For some time now I've known that it was coming and, to tell you the truth, I'm resigned to it and don't mind in the least, because it's time."

"Time, Father?" Eliza anxiously questioned. "Why do you say it's time? I don't understand."

Matthew Carson took a long breath and then gave a long sigh.

"I say it, Mary Eliza, because I actually stopped living some time ago. You see, I'm tired. I've become too tired to derive any pleasure from life anymore. So, you think about what I'm saying, dear, and dry your tears." He sighed once more. "I tried to make your Aunt Amy see how I feel about all this, but I fear all I did was upset her more than she is already. But I truly think you'll understand what I'm talking about. You do, do you not?"

His still deep blue eyes probed Eliza in earnest.

"I, I think I do, Father." Murmured Eliza. "But maybe if you'll just rest and do as Seth tells you, you'll …"

"No, dear," interrupted Matthew, finally lifting his hand and waving aside Eliza's remarks. "Seth's a good doctor, better than the average in my book, but reversing the ravages of time in this old worn-out body is far beyond his genius, I fear. Certainly, the feat of that kind of miracle is not to be found in Seth's tonic, because if it were, I'd already been made anew by this time or at the very least beginning to sprout a few new parts!"

The corners of his mouth curved upward, revealing a somewhat but weak impish smile.

Taking courage from his game and fearless attitude, Eliza smiled back with a weak smile, too, and bending forward and reaching for the hand that he had so feebly lifted and then let fall back on his chest, she said, "Oh, Father, you are truly some cut-up. No wonder poor Aunt Amy became a little put out with your attitude."

Taking time to inhale a few more deep breaths and then coming up once again with a strength of voice that Eliza thought surely belied the worldly time limit that Seth Roalf had set for her father, Matthew said, "Well, sometimes, dear girl, one must be realistic and stick to the facts and that's what I'm doing. In fact, I want you to do likewise, and also promise that you'll do your best to make your Aunt Amy understand what I was trying to get across to her. You will do that for me?"

Once again, his gaze probed Eliza's face.

"Of course, I will, Father," Eliza muttered, trying to deaden the sob gathering in her throat – "but please try to rest now. I'm afraid you're going to overtire yourself and bring on another attack."

"No, let me talk, dear, I assure you I won't do myself any harm, maybe some of my listeners, but certainly not myself!" He went on, the sound of his voice coming forth so easy and strong that it actually gave Eliza a start. "Heavens, even if my talking does bring on another fainting spell, I won't be that much worse off for wear and tear, believe me!"

"But, Father, you seem so much stronger, a great deal better than you were earlier today when I first saw you. I know Seth's tonic must be working this time, so please won't you try to rest and give it a chance to help you more than it already has," implored Eliza as she gently squeezed her father's hand.

"I'd say if I've rallied to any degree, dear," smiled Matthew. "It's not because of Seth's tonic, but due to that big swig of brandy that I asked Amy to pour me just before I insisted that she get out of here and go get some rest – shortly before I asked to see you in private."

"Brandy, Father?" questioned Eliza, her face registering a mark of disconcertion. "Does Seth know you're drinking brandy along with his medicine?"

"Well, if he doesn't dear, he's not quite as smart as I believe him to be, or either he can't smell, I wouldn't know which. Surely you must smell it. You do, do you not?"

"Well – yes," Eliza confessed. "But –"

"Oh, don't worry so, dear," interrupted Matthew for a second time. "Take my word for it, it won't be the brandy that'll finish me off. The evildoer is this old ticker of mine and the years of course. Still, I've made good use of my eighty-five years and don't you ever forget that. Sure, I've known sorrow

10

and also experienced the worst kind of grief. By the same token, I've harbored few regrets in my lifetime and known more happiness than most people come by no matter how long they live."

"I had the wisdom to make two good marriages, I did, something that most men don't come by within a mile of doing even on the first go around, let along the second!" Suddenly, Matthew ceased his talk and not only seemed to be lost in thought, but appeared to be seeing something that was visible to only himself. Finally, as Eliza continued to hold his hand and observe his seemingly pensive expression, he turned his head toward her and said, as another sudden lightness appeared on his face, "You know, although I've never told you till now, I've taken notice lately that your face has a lot of her in it. Yes, by Jove, I wonder why I didn't see it long before I did, because you do favor her a great deal! Yes, every day you grow older I can see it stand out more."

His scrutiny combed Eliza's features most attentively.

"Favor who, Father?" Eliza anxiously pressed. "I always thought I favored no one but you."

"Your mother, dear girl, that's who and don't you ever let anyone tell you that the resemblance isn't there just because they can't see it, for it's there alright and very defined at that. It's true, the Carson blood is most distinct in your face. On the other hand, that peaches and cream complexion and fine bone structure, the tilt of your chin and those high cheekbones came from no Carson. Take my word for it, that side of your looks came from no one but your lovely mother."

Suddenly, something seemed to have taken a stitch in Matthew Carson's voice. It threw a scare in Elize that she worked hard not to show as she said, "Yes, Mother was lovely and so graceful. I recall, it made no difference how trying or awkward the situation was, I don't believe I ever saw her lose her composure, not once, a characteristic that unquestionably gave her daughter the jump, because I confess. I become discomposed and have more times than I have fingers and toes.

"Well, even if you have and still do occasionally don't

discredit yourself, dear girl. Though your mother was grace itself that doesn't mean grace is all restraint and nothing else. It's many other things too like having polish and using good judgement and being morally decent and the like, all fine qualities you can claim as well as other creditable ones. So what if you do lose your cool on occasion? That doesn't mean you're not graceful. It merely shows you're high-spirited and nothing else. Therefore, you keep that in mind – and don't forget – it."

Once again voicing his words had suddenly become an effort for Matthew.

Instantly, Eliza was cognizant to the fact that her father had fallen from better to worse in a split second. It frightened her. Discarding the subject of taste and niceness from her mind immediately she said, as her face became heavy with alarm, "Father, maybe you'd better let me call Seth back in here to have a look at you and check out your medication again. He's just outside the door there talking with Phil and Luke. I'll go get him." She started to rise from her chair.

"No," he said, "and sit back down and stop your worrying. It's just a little pain that sorta grows sharper every now and then and catches my breath. It's nothing now and nothing for you to get alarmed about. Besides, I want to talk and telling me not to talk would be the first thing that Seth would say to me if he were in here. So let the doctor stay where he is, I'll be all right."

Though she very much doubted that his assurance was the straight truth because he wanted it that way, Eliza, yielding to his wishes, said, "you're sure?"

"Yes, darling," he smiled, "I'm sure." And then ignoring the dull chest pain that he had lived with for some time, not to mention his severe fatigue, he went on talking, telling Eliza as she reluctantly settled back down in her chair and tried to smile back at him, "You know it's truly incredible and especially since so many years have fallen between then and now, but I can see as clearly right now how your mother looked on the night we met as I could then. She was wearing a pink chiffon ball gown and had a nosegay of pink camellias pinned in her hair. Though she was not wearing one single trace of jewelry she was simple dazzling just the same. I – "

"Oh, Father," interrupted Eliza, eager to push her fears aside and absorb his every word, "I never knew that. You're telling me things I've never heard before. Pink. I remember it was Mother's favorite color."

"Yes, and I must say it was most becoming to her, too, suited her well. Anyway, I thought she was the most beautiful creature I'd ever laid eyes on. Of course, when I first spied her across the ballroom floor, I hadn't the foggiest notion who she was. But that was a funny thing, too, because just as I saw her and was wondering about her, actually praying that she was not already betrothed or worse still already married, she looked in my direction and as her eyes found mine and we stood there staring back at one another, I knew as surely as day is day that she was as free to pursue the impact of attraction generating between us as I was – free to love and be loved. And then, just at that moment and as incredible as it was, I heard Franklin saying at my elbow, "She's Anne Goodyear, Chap, the older of the Goodyear sisters and she's as free as you are, or at least I think she is! Want an introduction to check it out?"

Matthew suddenly let a slight chuckle roll and appeared to settle himself in a more restful position.

Observing the memory coming alive in his face, Eliza's optimism was on the rise again.

Echoing his little chuckle, she said, "And of course, you said yes and Uncle Franklin carried through. But tell me, just how did you and Uncle Franklin maneuver it? Surely, you two didn't defy custom and go bounding across the ballroom floor on the spot, or did you?" She became all agog with curiosity all of a sudden.

He sent her an incredulous look.

"Why, that is precisely what we did," he said, "It was an opportune time and I had no intention of letting it go by, mores or whatever."

Just like me so long ago at Windsor when propriety

happened to become my last care, thought Eliza.

She smiled, "But what astonishes me more than anything else is, although Uncle Franklin was already acquainted with Mother, he never suggested your meeting her till then. And what about Aunt Amy? I gather she was totally out of the picture at that time."

For a brief moment Matthew appeared to muse upon the question that Eliza had raised. Then he smiled, "No, Amy was very much in view, and I'm sure Franklin had his eyes upon her but doubtless at the time thought she was too young for him, because only one year later he certainly wasn't shy about going after her. To me, twelve months wouldn't have made that much difference, but to Franklin it made all the difference in the world, apparently. Regarding – " his voice trailed off for it another time, dashing Eliza's hopes to rock bottom.

"Father, please don't try to talk any more right now," she begged. "It's not that important – you can tell me later."

He took a deep breath and went on, "No, I must explain the other part of your question, you see, your Uncle Franklin had not known your mother that long a time, having met her the year before at the cotton exchange in New Orleans where he was conducting business with Anne's father, a cotton broker. Anne and Amy both had accompanied their father to his office that day. I suppose seeing me as a confirmed bachelor as he was himself, was why Franklin had stopped at trying to play the role of matchmaker between Anne and me or any other girl for that matter until he caught me staring at Anne looking as though I had become spellbound and to tell you the truth, I had."

"Oh, Father, even from the very beginning you loved Mother so," Eliza said, and thought to herself again, just like me when I saw Luke for the first time.

He smiled, his voice obviously encumbered by that stitch again, "Y-es, and let's not forget she was my first love too. Anne Goodyear Car-son – lovely An –."

A tearing pain had sliced through Matthew Carson's chest, the force of it cutting off the last thread of sound left in his voice and dimming the light in his vision to the dark of night as well. But then, upon the mere blinking of his eyelids, Matthew found the pain rapidly vanishing and saw by some wonderous miracle the dark was becoming all awash in glowing candlelight, and he was young again, skirting around on the ballroom floor on his agile legs and sure-footed stride toward the lovely Anne Goodyear. And, momentarily, he was planting a kiss upon the slender, dainty hand she had offered him, knowing as he did and as surely as day is day that they both were experiencing the birth of a long and enduring love for one another – this gift that God in His wisdom had given man and woman to share. And, taking in the warmth of her smile, Matthew Carson smiled back at her and gripped her hand more firmly than ever.

Startled at hearing her father's voice break off altogether as he was repeating her mother's name, Eliza jumping forward to the edge of her chair, cried, "Father!" Then, taking in the corpselike look suddenly spreading across his face, and at the same time telling herself not to panic, she heard herself cry once more, "Father," knowing full well that no sound was going to meet her cry aside from the rapid beat of her own heart drumming in her ears.

It had all happened so quickly. One minute her father was alive and talking. The next minute, as likewise to her mother that long ago day in New Orleans, shades of death were crossing his face. Of course, she had seen the look of death before and had known he was gone even as she had cried to him. Still, although she had expected his death, she had not expected the suddenness in which it had come. There had been no time to run for Seth, or no time to do anything else if anything could have been done. One second she was feeling the grip of his hand in hers, the next second a leaden lifelessness was replacing his grip.

She did not know why she felt compelled to still clutch her father's hand. She thought maybe the happy look on his face and the way his sightless gaze seemed to be so full of joy had something to do with it – her own way in not wanting to break the spell of his happy reminiscing – keep it alive as long as possible because it certainly had appeared that there at the last that it had become more to her father than just a memory. And perhaps it had. Who was to say?

Yes, it seemed as though that for her father the end was more like some joyous awakening to life rather than a parting from it. That was going to be her belief and what was going to sustain her in her bereavement. She supposed she should go tell Seth, who had treated her father with such lasting devotion for so many years, and all the others waiting in the hall, too, that he was gone. She must go and have a long talk with Aunt Amy also.

Looking down at her father's lifeless hand in hers, Eliza took it and gently placed it by his side on the bed. Then with a calm that she never would have dreamed meeting with in such circumstances, she opened the palm of her hand and tenderly brushed it over her father's eyes, finally closing his sightless gaze that was still locked to hers. She rose from her chair and, taking a long hard look at Matthew Carson's peaceful looking face and with a heavy heart and dry eyes as well, she turned and made for the door.

Though her marriage to Matthew Carson had lasted as long as the marriage between Matthew and her older sister – odd though it was Matthew Carson had enjoyed a twenty-four-year marriage with each sister – there was never any question in Amy Drakston Carson's mind as to where Matthew's remains should be interred. Of course, his remains, as likewise to her own which would be interred beside Franklin at Drakston Hall, would go home to Green Sea to lie beside Anne, Amy Carson had solemnly declared when she had perceived that everybody was waiting for her say-so before going ahead with the necessary steps regarding Matthew's burial. Yes, the grave was to be prepared immediately at Green Sea. Where else, pray tell? Amy had gone on to add in solemn earnest, showing once again that even in such grievous crisis she could still hold firm to that clear-sighted quality in her nature that Matthew Carson had perceived in her and had admired so.

Hence, on the following day, not only was Matthew's body taken to Green Sea and laid to rest in the Carson Cemetery beside his first wife, Anne Carson, but at Amy's request Matthew's funeral was conducted at Green Sea as well – a sorrowful and heartfelt occasion that in Amy's eye was to take on all the trappings of a revival meeting before the Reverend Marsh Reed saw fit to thunder his last prayer! Indeed, although she was deeply grieved and felt that all joy and laughter in her life had departed along with Matthew, Amy was not so consumed with sorrow and tears that the Reverend's tendency to forget about the real and sad element involved and preach instead on the evildoings of the members of the Baptist Church – not to mention the wrongs and evil habits of those of whom who were there to mourn Matthew did not escape her attention! As a matter of fact, Amy's ire in respect to Marsh Reed for near turning her husband's funeral into a revival for sinners was long subsiding within her! The Reverend's lack of polish in appearing to forget the honor and good words that he could have said about the departed had a deep impact on Amy so much so that it was some time before Marsh Reed was invited to relish another meal at Amy Carson's bountiful table at Drakston Hall! Still, Amy's disappointment with the Reverend was softened somewhat by reminding herself that doubtless Matthew would have been amused at Marsh Reed's tactics rather than offended had he been there.

However, swathed in black from head to toe – she even carried a black lace handkerchief – Amy held onto her stately manner throughout the whole ordeal, with nobody the wiser about her ire with Marsh Reed! But, even so, the word did circulate before it died away that Amy Carson had banished the Reverend from her table at Drakston Hall! And, in point of the black lace handkerchief, Amy was to carry black handkerchiefs for the remainder of her days. Actually, one might be inclined to think that Amy carried her devotion to Matthew's memory and her mourning him a little too far. For, besides never giving up the black handkerchiefs, she was to wear black for the rest of her life – the whole caboodle, hats, shoes, dresses, underthings, her entire attiring remained to be the color black!

Though Eliza did endeavor to carry through with her father's wishes that she accept his death and not grieve for him, she was weighed down with a deep and pervading sadness nevertheless – a heart grief so heavy that it seemed to totally overwhelm her will and strength no matter how hard she tried to concentrate on her father's last words to her and keep them in her thoughts. That is, this dark despondency had become the state of Eliza's feelings once she had reached Matthew Carson's burial site. For up until then the will and fortitude that had carried her from her father's deathbed and on through the ordeal of breaking the news to the other family members as well as Doctor Seth Roalf, not to mention the trial of telling her Aunt Amy and the talk she had promised her father she would have with the latter had held fast and firm with her. But then, like a shot, as she was standing under the magnolia tree that Luke had planted some years earlier between him and her Aunt Amy, her whole being suddenly became plunged into the darkest kind of despair. And the terrible part was its deep, desolating ache seemed to be totally separated from the grief she was suffering over the loss of her father! This mixture of emotions was so strange and novel that it actually startled her, urging her to grip onto Luke's hand all the harder, and for the first time in her life she found herself calling on that strength of sixth sense she knew she possessed to help her reason the feeling out – that clairvoyant insight that she would as leave she had never been born with. Still, for all its strength on other occasions, she seized upon nothing, no clouds, no visions, not one thing! In brief, there was nothing beyond the present proceedings of her father's interment.

She wondered if the memories of the young, vigorous and dynamic Matthew Carson were affecting her more than she realized and causing her to become more aware of the passing years. No, it was not that she minded the few gray hairs that time had planted on her head, but what did affect her and deeply at that was that Luke's once jet-black hair was almost white as snow! She still loved him so completely. Maybe the fear of Luke being taken from her and leaving her alone like her Aunt Amy was now was what had plunged her into such dark despair. Well, that was one fear she must not hold onto if she were to have any happiness at all and let it go right here right now at this cemetery. Yes, she must bury it and let it crowd her thoughts no longer. Yes, God and Heaven be praised, Eliza reminded herself, Luke was very much alive! And she must not give in to all this soul-hurting sadness plunging through every fiber that threaded her body and live in dread of meeting with grief at any given moment despite white hair, the mark of time that wrinkles show, slumped shoulders or anything else. For she must be positive and believe and trust that all was going to be well with Luke and herself for long years to come.

Eliza Heyward, edging closer inside the circle of Luke's protective arms about her waist and feeling their loving, spontaneous reflex as she did, not only became more determined and hard set against her fears on the instant but her hopes and faith too, regarding the years ahead became far more enduring.

Aside from that ever-present vacuum that Matthew Carson's death had created and left with his loved ones to endure, nothing else was to change or occur at either Drakston Hall or Green Sea that fall and winter to distinguish those seasons from other years. As expected, and most certainly the way the late Matthew Carson would have preferred it, life continued on and was to prevail with the daily routine and the normal run of things being no different than they had been on both plantations in past years.

As customary and while the greater part of the land lay fallow and untilled onto ground-breaking time in early spring, this was the time of year to cut and trim the overgrown hedgerows and ditch banks and clean out the ditches and spade them anew. It was also the season to gather and stack firewood that would cure next year's tobacco crop as well as the time of year to prepare and seed the tobacco plant beds, which was a must if one expected to farm the crop. However, these fall months were also the time of year to enjoy the sport of fox hunting – riding to the hounds among the Lowcountry gentry and with no class distinction involved. In addition, there was the sport of hunting for wild game in general, the huntsman thrilling to the hunt and delighting in the richness of it in the moonlit, frost-biting nights as much as the hounds did! And besides, the seasonal chores and sport of coursing with the hounds, the fall and winter months allowed one the time for other pleasures such as entertaining and visiting as well with family and friends. Still, above every sport or relaxation that the fall and winter provided one, nothing ever surpassed the installment of Christmas and Eliza was to make special effort that Christmas would be no different on this year from other years despite the missing presence of her father.

Of course, with her grandson Matt but a step away at any given time or at least within earshot, Eliza's endeavor to carry through turned out to be far easier than she had contemplated. For example, like cutting and bringing home the Christmas tree, an errand that Matt decided he was man enough to see to this year, and no amount of coaxing from his elders in respect to changing his mind did any good whatever.

So indulging Matt the errand of bringing home the Christmas tree was to become more than an errand for Luke and Eliza both before it was to end. For it turned out to be more like a hard days' work than anything else!

With Matt ensconced between them on the wagon seat – his round ruddy face looking ever as much as red in the biting December cold as the glowing holly berries flowering the unclothed land – Luke and Eliza and their charge, along with a basket of food packed against their becoming hungry before their return, set out early one morning for Green Sea's wooded acreage to find Matt's Christmas tree.

No, Luke did not head the wagon toward the old timber trail. Taking to that route would have risked setting both his and Eliza's calm too much as hazard. In brief, that one scenic place had bred too much grief and too many heartaches. So instead, Luke headed the wagon for another track of woods that, although may not have been so vividly striking with blooming holly trees offered as much in the way of wagon paths, because of the many paths that had been sliced through the woods hauling the firewood out, not to mention all varieties of native evergreens, as the old timber trail did. But, even so, the noon hour came upon them and they still had not found a Christmas tree! And, what's more, Luke and Eliza both had begun to wonder if they ever would find one.

The trouble was Matt. He appeared to not be able to make up his mind as to the kind of evergreen he really wanted. He had spotted several small pines and had given the word each time that that was the tree he wanted. Then the very second that Luke had raised the ax to chop the pine down, a shrill, "Stop Grandpa," had erupted from Matt's lungs! And, not only had he drawn the line, so to speak, in regard to the pines being cut, but he had also stopped Luke from cutting down a number of hollies and cedars he had spied and said he wanted.

Now, however, with all three sitting upon the wagon seat taking a breather from hunting Matt's Christmas tree as well as replenishing their empty stomachs with the tasty food that Eliza had packed such as ham sandwiches, hard-boiled eggs, roasted peanuts, shelled-out pecans, apples and raisin-filled tea cakes, not to mention a half gallon jar of water and milk too, it suddenly hit upon Eliza the remote distance from anything they sat and feasted and would be forced to back trail for miles over brambles and scrub wood when they did turn the wagon for home. So promptly she reasoned that it was time to stop pampering their grandson, Christmas tree or no Christmas tree! Besides, the December sun was growing paler by the minute and the air was growing colder too! She had no desire for them to be subjected to a cold rain much less a sleet storm and so far away from shelter.

Thus, delaying no longer and taking matters in hand, Eliza said, as she handed Matt another tea cake and a cup of milk to wash it down with, "Matt, dear, we won't be traveling any further out into this wilderness looking for a Christmas tree. After we finish eating our dinner we're going to turn back toward the house. So, if you want to have a Christmas tree for Santa to take his rest by when he comes to Green Sea next week, you must select one on our way back. Why not make your choice from one of those you've already said you wanted but stopped your grandfather from cutting, or let him select one for you? That way you won't be troubled about it any longer."

Eliza was certain that her suggestion had settled the problem. She soon saw that she had fixed not one thing though.

Munching away on his tea cake in silence Matt let Eliza's suggestion hang rather long. Then just when Eliza and Luke both were certain he was going to remain silent and say nothing, he said, as they both observed all light had left his face, "I'll pick it out, Grandmother, myself. I'll pick it out real soon, I promise."

Luke and Eliza both were puzzled by Matt's downcast look, with Eliza feeling that she had caused it by her suggestion to Matt. So, wanting to make amends for her say and perhaps lift her grandson's seemingly low spirit somewhat, she said, "Very well, Matt, but besides a Christmas tree we're going to need some greenery to decorate the mantles and tables with. I think holly might be best for that because of its red berries. Want to help me gather some holly? I've seen several holly trees with low-hanging branches that I'm sure you'll be able to reach."

She waited anxiously, hoping that Matt would show a little enthusiasm.

"Holly's pretty," said Matt and made no further comment. Nor did his put-out look change.

Luke turned the wagon around and headed it back over the wooded trail that they had already covered, passing by several evergreens that Matt had selected and said he wanted until Luke was ready to chop it down but Matt had stopped him. And Matt was continuing to hold his silence as well as his solemn look. Then, just as Luke and Eliza had begun to think their Christmas tree outing was going to come to nothing, Matt was suddenly crying, "Over there, Grandpa! There's my Christmas tree! Stop the wagon!"

Luke pulled on the horse's reins, looking around for Matt's Christmas tree but all he saw was a patch of small cedars that doubtless had seeded from the huge cedar tree that sheltered them. Surely his grandson had not chosen one of those, he was thinking but only had a second or two to entertain the question in his head. For Matt had already scrambled down from the wagon and was running over to one of the small cedars and exclaiming, "This is it, Grandpa! We can dig this one up with the shovel and not chop it down and kill it like Grandpa Matthew dying and buried in the ground!"

Startled beyond words and now perceiving what had troubled Matt from making a choice among the evergreens and having the tree chopped down, Luke and Eliza shared a meaningful look between them, with both thinking that no grownup ever knew what thoughts went on in a child's mind at any given time and especially in a family crisis or unexpected events! They both were seeing more deeply into their grandson's makeup, his sensitivity over the destruction of a living tree and promised themselves they would be more heedful of it in the future. Though it was becoming more difficult by the minute for them to vision the little cedar as Green Sea's Christmas tree that Christmas! For the one that Matt was standing by with a happy glow on his face was no more than a few inches above his head!

Making an effort to be as normal as possible and show no surprise at all in regard to the small cedar, Luke, jumping from the wagon, said, "Certainly, son, just give me a minute to get the shovel and we'll start digging it up. Actually, Matt, if we're really careful with its roots, I don't see why we can't keep it alive for some time to come. In fact, we may be able to set it out in the yard after Christmas."

"Oh, Grandpa," Matt was exclaiming again, his gaze dancing with excitement, "Do you reckon we can do that? Set it out!"

"Well, we can certainly give it a try, a chance to spread its roots again by keeping it as fresh and green as we can by putting it in a bucket of dirt and giving it plenty of water until

23

we set it out in the yard later," said Luke.

Eliza silently praising Luke for his wisdom and feeling her spirit building by the minute, too, scrambled down from the wagon and joining Luke and Matt at the little cedar as the process of removing it from the ground began, said, "Matt, we'll put the tree in a bucket and decorate the bucket with green crepe paper so it'll look more like Christmas. It'll also be your job to keep the tree watered until we do set it out in the yard. And, you may decorate its branches with a few Christmas items, too, if you like and always claim it as your tree, not only this Christmas, but for every Christmas that comes ahead of us."

Luke, lifting his head from his work and exchanging another meaningful look with Eliza as well as a highly pleased one too, said, before Matt so overwhelmed with all that was crowding his mind could speak, "What a great idea, Matt, your grandmother's come up with! All the more reason for us to hurry with keeping your tree green and healthy until we get it in a bucket of dirt. Besides, this weather is beginning to look more like sleet or snow by the minute!

Matt, with a grin from ear to ear was finally able to mouth some of his thoughts, saying "You bet Grandmother has, Grandpa! I can't wait to tell Frankie and Lizzie that I have my own Christmas tree and it's going to stay alive too! Oh, boy!"

Luke and Eliza were to exchange another knowing look.

Along with the little cedar wrapped snugly against the dislocation it had undergone and lying in the bed of the wagon, the Christmas tree hunting trio were also back on the wagon seat and headed for the shelter of home in record time and a good thing too. For within a short time, a few snowflakes were beginning to fall from the heavy leaden sky. And, by then, it also became obvious to Eliza and Luke both that Matt's arduous task that day had been a little too much for him due to his head falling forward with a nod on his chest every few seconds.

Eliza reached and lifted Matt upon her lap and gathered him close, telling herself that since the house was in sight and they would reach it in a few minutes she would arouse Matt then. Because she wanted Matt to know and experience the novel delight, wanted him to see the white, feathery snowflakes whirling and dancing around them and feel the thrill of their cool, soft kisses upon his cheeks.

Eliza Heyward was entertaining other thoughts in her mind too. She wondered and was seeing the falling snow as a good omen, a sign that their Christmas this year was going to be a good and joyful holiday in spite of the recent loss of her much-loved father. The fact was, she felt that Matthew Carson's namesake whom she held in her arms was going to make it so. Feeling her love for Matt, Green Sea's heir, coursing through her veins like the warmth of good vintage wine, she gathered him closer still and lifted her face into the refreshing wash of the snow.

And, as it was thus with Eliza, drawing a comfort of heart from Matt's presence and a renewal of spirit from the falling snow, it was likewise with Amy Carson at Drakston Hall. Seeing the snow peppering down, she had quickly donned a wrapper and thrown a scarf over head and made for the outdoors with Frankie and Lizzie. And, right away, not only had she become aware that she was laughing and playing in the snow with the children as though she were a child herself, but she suddenly began to view the remainder of her days as being far fuller and more enjoyable than what she had contemplated when she had stood and watched Matthew Carson's coffin lowered into its resting place at Green Sea some two months earlier.

Henceforth, the snowstorm came and went and so did a most joyous Christmas as Eliza had envisioned and surprisingly, with Matt's little cedar tree prevailing through both and by year's end he and his Grandpop Luke were to take much delight and pride from seeing the sturdy small tree obviously adjusting itself to its new location in the backyard at Green Sea.

The beginning of the new decade 1891 was to remain tranquil with no trouble marking it, nor for that matter, no great doings either. Then with the coming of spring – a time of flower-scented days and sunny heavens – Eliza's world seemed even more bright. For this was the season she loved best, a time of year that made her feel as though a bed of soft down was cushioning her constantly. And yet, even in this halcyon time of quiet and calm, Eliza Heyward found herself doing something one morning in early June – it appeared Eliza was all haste to ever find something to worry about regardless – that was totally outside her normal behavior and that was taking time during her daily toilette to study her reflection in the mirror!

As Eliza sat there at her dressing table taking in what the mirror was telling her, she did not become alarmed. Nor did she become distressed. On the other hand, she was far from starting to cheer either to note that she was no longer wearing the glow of her younger years. Moreover, she observed her face seemed fuller, more matronly-looking than what she had thought and, certainly, not as finely defined in bone structure as it was in her youth. However, leaning closer to the mirror and giving herself a more diligent scrutiny, she decided that the years had not been too cruel to her after all because she saw that her face was as free of wrinkles and crows feet as it ever was, doubtless due to having always shaded it with a sunbonnet or some other type of headgear when she had ventured outdoors. She saw that her deep-violet eyes and heavy dark brows were the same as far as she could tell, and she truly had to search and search hard to find the one or two gray hairs that she knew were in her head, which to her, was indeed a marvel considering the worrywart she was and the fact that come December she and Martha both would be counting their forty-eighth birthday! She could hardly fathom the reality of that fact and found herself almost shuddering at the thought of being only a couple of steps, so to speak, from the half century mark! She wondered how Martha felt about turning forty-eight, and thinking about the impulsive and headstrong Martha she smiled to herself.

It was only yesterday as she and Luke were sitting on the

porch talking that Martha had come tearing up the drive again with such force – almost running into the side of the house and scaring them half to death – that Luke had threatened to put a barricade up at the point where Martha turned onto the circular drive leading to the front steps to keep her off it! What had saved Martha from cracking her head on one of those oak trees long before now was a mystery to her anyhow, because Martha had always come tearing up that drive, and especially if she were upset about something, like a demon was chasing her.

She supposed one could say that Martha's actor son-in-law Cornwallis Silverspoon was the evil spirit chasing Martha yesterday! It appeared Martha put all the blame on Mr. Silverspoon for not having been informed that Laura was in the family way till the actual telegram from London, England, came yesterday announcing the baby's birth! Even though Mr. Silverspoon's telegram had been most cordial and newsworthy, stating that the baby was a boy and had been christened Randolph and both mother and son were fine and a long letter would follow shortly, Martha's ire with the actor had been no less wild and furious than had she read about the baby's birth in a newspaper. Indeed, Martha had sworn that she was barring Mr. Silverspoon from Oak Grove permanently. She very much doubted that Martha would go that far though even if she was mad as a hornet and chose to stay that way to boot!

At any rate, through Laura, Martha and Bruce had finally become grandparents. It looked as though Maggie and Seth Junior were going to remain childless. Maggie was already thirty-one years old and no baby yet. How strange it was about Elms anyway? Of all the many footsteps sounding throughout its wide halls day in and day out not a single one was the footsteps of a Wilton, or for that matter, the footstep of anybody who carried one drop of Wilton blood in their veins.

She was so grateful that Green Sea was going to be spared that kind of fate – no Carson heirs to inherit it. It had come so awfully close though to be just like Elms. With Luke and herself remaining childless so many years, the war taking Nat's life, not to mention Phil listed missing in action at Gettysburg and ultimately taken for dead for a period of twenty-one years, she regarded it as more than a marvel that the Carson bloodline had not come to a finish altogether. But, thank God, it had not and Matt was living proof of that with his Carson blood manifesting it so boldly in his facial features every time she looked at him. No, the fact that Matt's surname was Heyward instead of Carson did not disturb her in the least. Indeed, since it was Heyward money that had saved Green Sea from those heinous Carpetbaggers, she thought it only right – actually rather fitting – that the heir to Green Sea did turn out to be a Heyward! Besides, not only was Heyward an old and honorable name, but Matt and his father before him had come by the name through a man who instead of touting his Christian qualities – a common habit of most churchgoers – let them show by the way he conducted himself and lived his life from day to day.

Yes, if anybody had ever measured up to being a true Christian, Luke was that person – a firm believer of love for family and friends and doing charitable deeds for his fellow man. Therefore, in her eye, the name Heyward was going to be an asset to Green Sea doing it as proud as the name Carson ever had!

Suddenly, at the sound of Luke's feet bounding up the stairs – yes having listened for Luke's footsteps so many times through the years she could tell them from no other – Eliza let her spinning thoughts go and anxiously turned her head toward the door. She wondered what had brought Luke back to the house so early and regretted that she had dallied so long at the mirror that he was going to see her hair still undressed and hanging loose instead of brushed and arranged on her head in the style of a coronet like she had worn it for years.

"Anything wrong, Luke?" she quietly asked as he bolted through the doorway.

"Not one thing, I'm happy to say," he smiled, coming on across the room to where she sat. "I see you aren't dressed yet. Aren't you feeling well?" His smile faded in instant concern.

"Oh, I'm alright, Luke," she promptly assured, "I've just

let my thoughts carry me off a little too far from my duties, I suppose."

"That's my doll," he smiled again. "Forever letting her mind spin with something."

"I won't join issue with that," she smiled back. "But tell me, why have you come back to the house so early? You usually stay in the fields till dinner time."

"I came back to see if I could talk you into going for a horseback ride with me, just us, Mrs. Heyward, and no one else. I showed the hands how I wanted the tobacco plowed, so there's really nothing else pending today that I can think of. What do you say? It's such a beautiful morning, and to tell you the truth, I can't even recall the last time we took a horseback ride together just for pleasure."

"I won't argue that point with you either," she said. "But I don't know, Luke, I had planned to do some baking this morning, make a batch of pies out of those huckleberries that the hands picked and brought to the house yesterday. They said the woods are simply packed with them this year." A teasing smile suddenly curved her lips. "You do relish fresh huckleberry pie, do you not? If I remember correctly, you near ate a whole one when I baked the first batch last season."

"So, I did," he grinned, "but I relish pleasurable horseback rides, too, and especially with you. Besides, can't Pete or Bessie see to the huckleberries? And, what about Beth Anne? It's my understanding she doesn't mind one bit to get a little flour on her elbows."

"No, let it be flour or anything else, she appears not to mind one bit," said Eliza, "but she's busy helping Carr this morning with his paperwork. And Bessie is busy with housework and Pete already has enough on his hands with clearing breakfast away and making preparations for dinner." She paused suddenly looking thoughtful. "I guess it wouldn't hurt to let the baking go till this afternoon, but look at my hair, Luke, it'll take me over thirty minutes to do anything with it, let along the time to get into my riding habit."

"Well, we'll take care of your hair right this minute," said

Luke, reaching for the wide blue silk sash that adorned her dressing gown and pulling it loose. "Here, tie your hair back with this."

He dangled the sash in front of her.

"Luke, you can't be serious," she laughed, "suggesting that I tie my hair back and it so long that I could actually sit on it? And furthermore, I'm not sixteen, you know!"

"You are to me and always will be, no matter what your age is." Luke said, and setting his gaze on a direct level with hers, he went on, "Now take this sash and tie your hair back so it won't be blowing in your eyes, and I'm going on and ready our horses!"

Seeing the earnestness in his gaze, she demurred no longer, saying as she reached and took the sash from his hand, "Give me a few minutes and I'll be there."

Presently, as Luke was waiting for Eliza beside the saddled horses – noting as she came toward him the sleekness of her figure under her riding habit as well as how fetching her long hair looked hanging down her back between two long blue streamers – it was hard for him not to think that she was hardly more than sixteen instead of the forty-eight-year-old woman she was. In fact, his mind suddenly went back to that day at Windsor when he first saw her and told himself that the years had actually added to her uncommon beauty rather than faded it.

"You make a rather fetching picture, Mrs. Heyward," he said, offering her his hand and helping her mount.

"Then, I won't have to concern myself with the possibility of your becoming bored," she quipped, smiling down at him as she settled herself in the saddle.

"Bored, and you looking all of sweet sixteen and fresh as paint? I should think not, Mrs. Heyward," he shot back. And then after raking her over with a rather long and roguish gaze, he turned and swung upon his own mount.

Pacing their horses at an easy gallop and with Eliza, deliberately, letting Luke take the lead by restraining her mount somewhat as they came to the end of the oak-lined avenue they hit the river road and headed their mounts in a southward direction. Luke charging this direction instead of heading north toward Drakston Hall or Oak Grove surprised Eliza. For they were bound to come to the overgrown fifty acres, which Early Cole had owned and which he also had termed a prosperous plantation rather often before he let it go to weeds and brush and finally losing it to Frank Drakston to boot. In addition, the old moldy, weed-choked cabin that Early had also called a manor house from time to time was still partially standing though it was grotesquely bent and weather-beaten by time and the elements but hanging on by a few durable posts and boards and looking for all the world like some gray-shrouded ghost who was stubbornly refusing to accept its untimely and unfortunate fate certainly, it happened to be one landmark that Eliza would have guessed that given a choice, Luke would have skirted for miles!

Still, Eliza called no verbal attention to her thoughts, choosing instead to push the troubles of other days aside and concentrate on matters at hand. Besides, she was wise enough to know that she had too much to be grateful for than to let her appreciation of it be reduced by looking back on past ordeals. And the truth of that fact had never been more perceptible to her than on this balmy and luminous June morning.

On no occasion could Eliza recall that a mere horseback ride had ever felt so invigorating to her – the freshness of the morning's air kissing her cheeks and her senses so tuned to the lush and abounding greenness covering the land that she felt as though her very soul was set to notes of sweet music playing a song of jubilation and praises to all the loveliness before her – the dew-capped and daisy-spotted pasture field where Bullitt was leisurely grazing and so many years up in age that he was seldom harnessed nowadays, the wide flourishing cornfields and acre upon acre of thriving, velvety-green tobacco rows, all of it pulsing through every fiber of her being. But above and beyond everything her senses were attuned to the one thing that exceeded all else was her love for the man riding beside her, yes, despite all the ups and downs that she and Luke had encountered and experienced together she took deep joy and gratitude to acknowledge that not only was her love for him as vibrant and pulsing as ever, but to also feel that his devotion for her was no different and as alive as it ever was.

All at once, as Eliza and Luke were leaving the ruins of the old Early Cole cabin behind them, it came to her that they were near the place where the glade that she used to visit long years back was and she wanted to visit it again with Luke.

Turning her head toward him, she asked, "Where are we headed to? Any place in particular?"

"No, not really, unless you'd like to gallop on to Charleston," he said, with a teasing smile as he kept his mount alongside hers in a slow walk.

"Oh, be serious, Luke. In the first place, you know Charleston is too far from here to go by horseback, -- well, if one has other means of travel anyway, and if that were not the case with us at present, you should know I'd never be so forward as to go tearing through its streets on a horse's back!"

"I don't see why not, being the skillful horsewoman you are," he teased again. "But, since you won't consider going on to Charleston, I suppose we'll just stick with the present scenery unless you have something else in mind, do you?" he said, his smile turning into a wide grin.

"Well yes, as a matter of fact, I do," she promptly replied.

"And what is that?" he asked, his grin growing wider.

"I want to see the glade again, the glade on the riverbank," she said, looking into the distance.

"The glade on the riverbank," he echoed, dropping his grin. "I didn't know there's a glade on the riverbank. I've never heard you speak of it before."

"That's because I've seldom given thought to it over the years. Long before I met you, I discovered it one day when I went swimming in the river. From then on it became a special place for me. I visited it time and time again. It was such a restful and pretty place, nothing growing on it but grass. I'm almost certain it was the site of an Indian settlement long ago, although I never saw any arrowheads. I'd tie my mare to a tree limb close by and lie down on the grass and let my imagination run wild, seeing the Indians dance their war dance and listening to the birds chirping and observing other wildlife that happened to venture nearby and feeling free as the birds and giving no thought to time either."

"You make it sound like it was pretty close to Eden or something near it," said Luke.

Still looking into the distance her gaze became dreamlike as she said, "Come to think of it, I guess it was. Maybe it still is, want to go and see?"

She turned her head and looked at him in expectation.

"Well, that depends," Luke came back, sounding none to eager. "Is it easy to ride to, a trail or something? Also, we must remember, dear, that what was a glade in years back in this part of the country could very well have turned into a thick-growing jungle by this time."

"That is a possibility, Luke, but with this particular place, I hardly think so. You see, in all those years before I discovered it, nothing had grown on it but moss and grass. I'm inclined to think that with the daily hum of the Indians living pattern as well as their war dances upon it that the ground was simply packed too hard and became too barren to sprout much growth of anything on it. No, there's no trail to follow, but I did have a marker that told me where to turn off from the road to find it."

"What kind of marker and where is it?" asked Luke, as he shifted his gaze from Eliza to scan the wooded acreage around them.

"See that big sycamore tree yonder not too far back from that ditch," said Eliza, thinking the ditch that separates the land of Green Sea from Early Coke's shabby acreage, "Well, we turn off the road from that spot and keep going straight ahead through the woods about a quarter of a mile."

"M-hmm," Luke grunted, appearing to have little interest in the venture. Then he turned to her and added with a smile, "I wonder what you'd do for a marker to go by if some misfortune had swiped your sycamore from the landscape in the meantime. But never mind that, Mrs. Heyward, if you say that's the turning off place and will stay in the lead, I'll put myself at your disposal and we'll begin the hunt for your glade."

"Of course, Mr. Heyward, I'll be most happy to stay in the lead, thank you," sniffed Eliza. Then she too took on a smile and added, "You won't be disappointed, I promise."

"Well, that being the case, let's stop the discourse and get a move on," said Luke, and giving his mount full rein, they both went sailing off toward the sycamore tree.

Keeping on a straight course through woods and numerous undergrowth that she had not ventured into for long years proved far more difficult than Eliza had foreseen. However, with Luke following close behind her, she was determined to stay it out and keep moving on the zigzag course that she was on because of the dense undergrowth that she had not counted on. Finally, when she was certain they had covered a quarter of a mile or near it and had seen nothing that had any looks of being anything but the forest it was, she was almost ready to admit defeat and suggest they turn back when a patch of overlarge bayberry trees jogged a chord in her memory!

Elated with the joy she felt at being pretty sure she had led them in the right direction, Eliza turned, looking back over her shoulder at Luke – whose expression told her that he was feeling anything but glee – said, "I'm certain it's just beyond these bayberry bushes, but we're going to have to dismount and lead the horses through them rather than try to ride through." She sailed from the saddle and grabbed hold of her mount's bridle.

"If you say so, dear," muttered Luke, his voice sounding dry as a desert as he also leapt to the ground to comply with her suggestion!

All the same, if her husband's fallen expression and dry tone of voice bothered Eliza, she never let on. Indeed, as she quickly stepped forward and peeked through a thick-leaf bayberry branch and saw the open glade she was too delighted as well as proud of her sense of direction to let something as trivial as Luke's obvious displeasure as having no road to follow needle her.

"Oh, Luke, it is the glade and it looks as though it's hardly changed at all!" she cried, hastily tearing on into the glade through another spot that was less obstructed by oversized limbs with her mount in tow.

Continuing to keep fast on Eliza's heels, Luke, swiftly replacing his fallen expression with one of newfound interest as his gaze fell upon the area, said, "Well, I must admit it does have all the looks of being rather quaint, and especially for an area so close to a river flow." He suddenly bent down and picked up an object near the toe of his boot and fingering it, he went on, "I think your belief of what this place once was is right on target, my dear, for here's your arrowhead!" He laid the old weatherworn object in her hand.

"Well, did you ever!" exclaimed Eliza, giving the ancient Indian object a close scrutiny. "Of all the times I came here I never saw a one, and the minute you step in here you're laying one in my hand. I can't believe it!"

"Maybe because I found it, I was on the lookout for one like I was on the watch that day at Windsor for a pretty girl like you," smiled Luke. "And pretty or otherwise, you found her and I'm thankful for that, not to mention your charm and your flattery, too, of course," quipped Eliza. Then laying the arrowhead back in his palm, she smiled and added, "Here, stick this in your pocket and we'll give it to Matt."

"Good idea," he said, slipping the arrowhead inside his trouser pocket. Then scanning the glade once again with mounting interest he, too, took on a smile and added, as he reached for the reins of her mount, "I'll tether the horses so we can rest a spell."

Falling down on the sun-splashed carpet-like grass and watching Luke proceed with securing their horses to a nearby tree, Eliza began to feel as though she were reliving all the glories of that other long ago June day when she had known she had lost her heart to Luke Heyward. To her, there might have been no time whatever falling between that day and this so all absorbing and unchangeable her love for him was. And eying Luke still as he retraced his steps and fell down beside her – stretching out on the grass full length with his hands locked under his head – she wondered if the glade's nostalgic setting was causing him to look back too.

It was only one brief moment before she found out! Suddenly, he was turning to face her and saying, as he raised up and propped is head on his elbow, "Now if we had a backdrop of the Blue Ridge lying off there just beyond those bayberry trees to gaze at while we have a go at becoming acquainted with one another again, everything would be just about as perfect as it was when we stopped to take a breather on that hilltop at Windsor that day."

Though she knew from the looks of Luke's expression that he could not have been more serious, the thought of either of them learning something about the other that was not already known to them amused Eliza.

She laughed, "Pray tell me, Luke, after all this time what on earth would you expect to discover about me that you haven't already made your acquaintance with long back?"

"Oh, lots of things," he readily smiled, reaching out with his free hand and giving her chin a little tug. "Aren't you aware that you keep me in a continuous state of expectation, ever wondering what's turning in that pretty head of yours, or what you're going to do next like coming here today, for instance?" His smile grew wider, "Not that I'm complaining though, keeps our marriage from growing stale!"

"Oh, come now, Luke," she said, pursing her lips in a little pout. "you make it sound as though I'm some frivolous or giddy sort, which I'm not and you know it! Besides, speaking of surprises, if I remember correctly, you've sprung a few yourself like never showing your face that night at Windsor when I had taken the pains to look my very best just for you. Never was I so disappointed in anybody. I've never forgotten it!" Verbally recalling it had sent her voice rising on a high note of indignation.

"I was a fool, and I've never forgotten it either," said Luke, instantly drawing his smile in.

"You haven't?" Eliza muttered, thinking no more of her ire as she lifted her brows in surprise.

"No, I haven't," Luke maintained, "because not only was it pigheaded of me to let all those precious hours go to waste, but it also came darn close costing me the pain of never winning you besides. I did, eventually, get around to straight thinking though and I've always been grateful that I did."

"So have I, Luke," Eliza said, and as more verbal confessions fell between them, an unusual airing of their feelings over matters long past with both becoming to feel as though they were clasped to the other in a loving embrace. And more talk fell between them on different subjects that differed not too much from that which might have passed between two people getting to know one another better after all, covering periods in both their lives that they had never talked about before.

They continued to talk on, talking about their meeting one another at Windsor, their marriage, the birth of their two children, their children's marriages, their grandchildren, the good and happy times they had experienced together as well as the bad and dark times too, recalling everything in shared ease and trust. Then as the seemingly heavenliness of their surroundings continued to hold them in a blessedness of closeness, their talk reverted back to Windsor on a certain day and hilltop where lightning might have flashed and thunderbolts burst so electrifying the pull of attraction was between them and still was!

Luke, his voice suddenly becoming husky, said, "But that was then, sweetheart, and this is now, the present. So, let's not waste the opportunity to make it count."

He raised himself to a sitting position and opened his arms to her.

Making no mistake about the kind of invitation her husband was extending to her, Eliza slightly blushing, said, as she cast her eyes in another direction to avoid his gaze, "It might be better if we continue on with our chitchat, Luke. This Eden doesn't have walls, you know."

"True enough," agreed Luke, "but it does have a pretty woman sitting here amid its bliss and that's the important thing or at least to me it is, not walls! Besides I should think the quaintness of these surroundings and the originality involved would banish all thoughts for the privacy of board walls anyhow." His comment had bordered on the tone of keen disappointment!

"Some could see us," she said, her pulse beginning to quicken at the thought of his suggestion.

"You worry too much," he came back.

"No doubt about that," she readily agreed, as she brought her gaze back to meet his. "Perhaps I could change though."

"Yes, perhaps you could," he smiled, and seeing that her concern over the privacy of walls was counting no longer with her, he shifted his position and closing the space between them he went on to see to it that time, walls or anything else was to exist for either of them but their intense love for one another, feelings that were to generate such a sweet harmonious song that it seemed as if its throbbing beat was still holding them in its swaying rhythm even after the music had stopped.

Some long minutes later, Luke, propping himself on his elbow again, said, "It's incredible. Although you are indeed a worrywart, I don't see one gray hair in your head."

Still looking in a dream-like state stretched out alongside him, Eliza lazily muttered, "That's because, dear husband, you aren't looking very hard because they're there alright. In fact, it was only this morning that I found myself counting them."

"And what was your tally, one or maybe two? I'm certain you had to search and search hard at that to even find that many."

"Not as hard as you think with them blazing first thing in the mirror when I looked in it," muttered Eliza again, though the tone of her voice sounded as indifferent had they been discussing which way the river flowed.

"The deuce you say! Surely you don't expect me to believe that," Luke said. "Wait until you're white as I am before making remarks like that."

Suddenly, Eliza was wide awake and bringing herself to a sitting position.

Regarding Luke with a most attentive eye, she said, "This is the first time I've ever heard you say one word about your hair being gray. The fact is, since you're still as handsome as you were the day I met you, you can't be bothered about your hair not being black anymore. Besides, even if you had no hair at all my love for you would remain the same as ever."

Luke smiled, "Of course, it doesn't bother me, dear, and thanks for the soft words. It's only what it does remind me of when I observe how gray it is, is what concerns me."

"And what is that, if I may ask?" pressed Eliza.

Time, love, time and how fast it's passed," said Luke. "And the thought of how you'd make out if I were no longer around. Certainly, my deepest hope is that you'd carry through and live a normal life and not by any means become a nonbeing, so to speak. We must acknowledge that I am the older by several years, you know."

All at once, for Eliza, the balmy June day might have been one in darkest winter so cold and desolate she had become. Still, determined to overcome the feeling and not give in to whatever peril her sixth sense was threatening to hurl at her, she forced herself to laugh and said, "You make it sound as though you're about to become as old as Methuselah. Well, nine hundred sixty-nine years like him, eight years, the eight years between us, or no age at all, we're going to be together for long years yet. Actually, I feel by our coming here today and being alone together like this is the beginning of a new phase in our lives, the beginning of our seeing to it that we make more time for our being alone together like we are now, just the two of us and just for the pleasure of it and nothing else. Let's do it, Luke, make a pact to slip back to this place as often as we can. Don't you agree?" She anxiously waited for his response.

"Wholeheartedly," smiled Luke, "and especially, Love, if you make our future trips back here together as interesting and delightful as you have today!"

Trying to hide the deep blush that was covering her face, Eliza dropped her head and said, "Luke, don't tease, I'm serious."

"So am I, Love," he teased again, and bending forward he planted a kiss on her flaming cheeks.

Chapter Two

As fate would have it, Eliza was never to visit the glade again. For the remainder of that entire summer and well on into the months of autumn – an ideal time to have paid a visit back – it seemed the chance of her and Luke seeking the privacy of the wooded, primitive setting once again to take delight in and enjoy together was always within their reach, but at the same time forever eluding their grasp. In addition, if the weather was not the holdup, some duty or responsibility was to either of them and oftentimes both of them in these two busy seasons. Then, by the time all the crops were harvested and seen to, the holiday season was upon them and the business of making ready for both Thanksgiving as well as Christmas. Even if they had had the time or the urge to visit the glade from time to time on a balmy day during the holiday season, the joy and satisfaction they both took from preparing for both holidays easily pushed the thought aside to some other time. Thus, taking the time to visit the glade was put on the shelf, so to speak. And, so often as some plan may come to nothing, the holiday season and all the merrymaking and family get-togethers was all over with but fond memories of it, winter had come to the land and going to the glade then much less relaxing in the cold, stark nakedness of it, to say nothing of making love there was out of the question!

However, just because the intoxicating atmosphere of the glade was no longer at their disposal, that did not mean that the Heyward's love-making had ceased to take place. Because it had not! Granted, in the seclusion and warmth of their winter bed, their love and need of one another still endured and burned as ardently as it had in the glade or anywhere else for that matter.

Since the beginning of winter, the weather had been nothing but average temperatures. No severe cold had blown in. Nor had the season brought any ice, sleet, or snow to the region. Then, time was counting the last days of February from the calendar and, with the weather continuing to remain on the mild side, the local planters and sharecroppers alike had begun to turn their minds to the task of breaking ground and getting various seed supplies together and ready for the coming annual crops. And never idle and more than eager to start another crop year, it was to be expected and no accident that Luke's mind was centered on planting time, too, as he was making his way from the barn back to the house early one morning in late February, as was his habit and had been for several years to go to the barn first thing to check on the aged Bullitt and carry the stallion his usual treat of sugar balls.

Now entering the kitchen and seating himself at the breakfast table, Luke began to share his thoughts with Eliza as she filled his coffee cup and then took her own chair opposite him.

"Yes," he went on saying, "since the mild weather has been with us for so long and looks like it's going to continue to hold, I think I'll take the buggy and drive over to Georgetown today to get another sack of sweet corn seed. We're going to need it when we do start planting."

"But that will be the first of April, Luke, most likely, and that's weeks away," reminded Eliza. "Besides, before going to the barn a while ago, you said you believed you were getting the sniffles, so why not wait till later in the week anyhow. This weather could change, you know, and if it does you shouldn't run the risk of being caught out in it in an open buggy."

Sending Eliza a smile over his coffee cup, he said, "Your coffee has already taken care of my cold symptoms, so don't worry any more about that. Want to drive over with me, or do you feel you have to be here in case this is the day that Martha decides to bring that load of quilt scraps that I overheard her telling you about Sunday at church? I heard you promise her you'd help her piece them together."

"Yes, I did promise, and as much as I'd like to break it and go with you, I guess I'd better not. If she came and found me gone, I'd never hear the last of it." Grimacing with a sigh, Eliza went on, "She's got it in her head that the two of us can piece a whole quilt together in one day! Have you ever heard such nonsense?"

"No," smiled Luke, "considering the fact that I know there's going to be more talk going on than work once Martha gets here." He rose from his chair and walked over to the coatrack and took down his hat, adding, "I'd better get started so I'll be back long before dark. Bye, dear, and don't forget to tell Martha to remind Bruce about our monthly Hunters Club meeting this coming Friday."

Seeing that he was going out the door without taking his heavy-weight jacket with him, Eliza jumped up and, snatching the jacket from the coatrack, she cried, as she ran after him, "Here, Luke, take your heavy jacket! If the weather changes you'll need it!"

He turned back and taking the coat from her and throwing it over his arm, he smiled, "Always worrying about something," and brushing her cheek with a kiss, he stepped on through the kitchen door and on down the outside steps.

Regretting her promise to Martha more than ever, Eliza stood in the doorway and stared at his back until he had rounded the edge of the yard out of sight.

The mild, balmy weather appeared to hold with little change until around the noon hour. Then, already out of humor with herself – and Martha too – because it was apparent by then that Martha had chosen to sew the quilt scraps another day, Eliza had just taken her final look for Martha's buggy coming up the driveway when she observed the house felt a lot colder than it had earlier. She had paid no attention to feeling chilly or anything else due to her disappointment over Martha not showing up to piece quilt scraps. Turning back to take another look through the glass panels on either side of the front door, she became astounded to see the sky had already changed its color from bright blue to a cold looking steel-gray while the live oaks on the drive were tossing their limbs every which way in a northeast wind, a sure sign that a winter storm had begun to blow in with Luke caught out in it someplace, she was thinking as she retraced her steps back to the kitchen to ask Pete to lay a fire in the downstairs fireplaces

Now worrying about Luke, on top of her disappointment how the day was turning out, and holding no prospect that the weather was going to change back to the mildness of early morning, Eliza decided to work on her own quilt scraps, telling herself that keeping busy at something might settle her mind as well as her wrought-up nerves somewhat. Hence, settling down beside the warmth of the kitchen fireplace, she began to ply her needle in and out through the scraps of material. Still, for all her skill with the needle with the sewn quilt patches beginning to add up, her mind was not with what she was doing. It was centered on Luke and nothing else. Her only comfort, for what little it was, her knowing that he did have his heavy jacket which she had insisted he take with him.

Suddenly, the sound of driving sleet hitting against the windowpanes brought Eliza's head up with a jerk. Startled, she jumped up and, rushing across the floor to look outside, she became even more aghast to see sleet raining down so heavy and thick-packed that it reminded her of sifting white corn meal through a sieve. Never could she recall seeing the weather go from one extreme to the other so quickly. Just this morning, she and Luke had sat in a splash of spring-like sunshine at the breakfast table and talked of spring planting. Now, only a few hours later, he was out there someplace trying to make it home through a blinding sleet storm!

She heard the sound of footsteps entering the kitchen and turned from the window to see Carr and Beth Anne. As likewise with her and her sewing, the suddenness in which the sleet storm had hit had also interrupted them from the pile of paperwork that they were busy working on in Carr's law office.

However, if Carr were entertaining any doubt as to how his mother was feeling about the severe change in the weather, seeing her standing at the window with a quilt patch clutched in her hand dissolved it on the spot as he asked, in a forced offhand manner, "Did Papa say what time we should expect him back, Mother?"

"He mentioned something about early afternoon, which has already come and gone, and he's not home yet." She turned, and resumed gazing through the window at the driving sleet.

Still trying to play his own feelings down and not cause his mother further anxiety, Carr said, "One doesn't cover ground very fast in weather like this, Mother, we must give him time. Besides, Papa always plays it safe anyway. Not only will he ponder the situation and do what's best for himself, but he'll also consider his horse's well-being as well."

Phil Carson, who had been in the library since the dinner hour penning a long letter to Gilford and Lucy Sloan in Lexington, came bounding into the kitchen on Carr's last words. And agreeing with what he had overheard, he enjoined, "Carr's right, Eliza. Luke will know what's best to do and he'll do it. In fact, I think if the storm's as bad where he is as it is here, he'll hole up at some farmhouse along the way until weather conditions are more favorable. He won't try to drive on home in a hard sleet storm."

"I don't know," Eliza muttered. "I hope he won't, but I just don't know." She stopped at saying more, stopped at saying the one thing she was troubled over more than anything else and that was she knew Luke was not feeling his normal self when he had left home that morning. Yes, despite his assurance to the contrary, she was certain he was coming down with a cold or maybe even the grippe and the bitter cold weather was certainly not in his favor. And continuing to look through the window, she stubbornly refused to let the thought of the dread word pneumonia enter her mind. Granted, she could think in terms of Luke coming down with a cold or the grippe, but the worst winter malady of all, the dread pneumonia, never!

Though it was true that Luke was and had ever been the prudent and thoughtful person his son and Phil Carson had deemed him to be, on this day as he began to cover ground on his return home from Georgetown, taking refuge at some farmhouse from the bitter cold and driving sleet that had overtaken him never crossed his mind. His one and foremost thought was to reach Green Sea and hurry on to bed where he could finally surrender himself to the fact that he had indeed become ill, and at the very least would be relieved from wondering any longer if he were going to hold out to reach home or not!

Of course, Luke did feel for his horse and deeply regretted he was forced to head the animal on into the blinding sleet. But he pushed on home toward Green Sea because by this time he knew he had come down with something, and its symptoms were far more severe than that of a cold or maybe the grippe. Therefore, home was where he wanted to be. Besides, even if he had considered stopping at some farmhouse, his genetic makeup would have dismissed the thought on the spot since he had no idea what the nature of his illness was, and he would not have taken the risk of exposing anyone to some highly contagious disease he may have fallen victim to.

Luke's decision to journey to Georgetown that day to purchase farm seeds for spring planting could not have been more misjudged. For he was only a few short miles from reaching his destination when two things became apparent to him. First, despite his assuring Eliza that her coffee had restored the bad feeling that he had awakened with that morning was way off the mark, because he had begun to feel worse than ever. Second, the mild weather that he had envisioned remaining to hold through the entire day was no longer mild. Indeed, it had changed, and changed rapidly at that. The fact was, it had turned from mild to bitter cold in only a few hours. Grateful that Eliza had insisted he take his heavy jacket with him, he reached for it where it lay on the buggy seat beside him and put it on, and suddenly, became more thankful for its warmth because he began to shake with a hard chill. Though the chill finally subsided, it left him feeling feverish as well as wise to other surfacing symptoms such as pain in his chest when he breathed, which, of course, made him aware that he had become ill with something and wondered if he should proceed on for Georgetown or turn around and head for home. Still, with the city within his sight, he decided to journey on to James Mallory's seed and farm supply store.

Having done business with James Mallory, the proprietor of the store for long years, Luke and the farmer were certainly no strangers to one another and took much delight in the other's company. But on this day, after he had given the store owner his order for supplies and seeds, Luke appeared to have no urge to engage in a conversation as well as in a hurry to leave for home as quickly as possible, a manner that was entirely outside his normal behavior to James Mallory.

All the same, the store owner continued to get Luke's order together even though he kept his eye cocked in Luke's direction, and in so doing came to the conclusion that Luke Heyward was far from feeling well!

So, venturing to search out his sudden belief further, James Mallory said, "I hear there's a lot of sickness hereabouts. Must be something to it, because until you walked in here not one customer had I seen today. Of course, with the weather being so changeable, spring one hour and winter the next, it's no surprise to hear about people falling sick, or for that matter, taking much interest in being prepared for spring planting. Naturally though, as likewise to your many other worthy qualities, Luke, you're the ever exception."

"Perhaps, James, when it comes to trying to be ready to start another crop year. But regarding to those who aren't patronizing your business today because of sickness or otherwise, I'm afraid if I were where I should be, I'd be home, too, instead of here purchasing seeds. I can't recall when I've felt worse. About got my order filled and ready to go?" Luke asked.

Giving Luke another scrutiny as he tied a string around a bag of seed, James said, "Sure thing, this finished your order, and I'll load it for you. But listen, since you're feeling so poorly, are you sure you even want to start back home? It is quite a few miles you know, and this weather is getting worse by the hour. You'd be more than welcome to stay over at my place, your horse and gear too. I'd enjoy your company"

"No, I'd better not, James, I must get on home, but thanks for the offer, anyway," Luke said.

"Well, if you feel you must. How about downing a stiff drink before you start then? I have plenty of spirits in the back. It'll only take me a minute to fetch it. Have a favorite? It could brace you a little against that weather out there." James started to make a move for the back of the store.

Swiftly laying his hand on James Mallory's arm to restrain him though, Luke managed to smile and said, "No, James, and no favorite either since I hardly know one brand from the other. You see, I made such a fool of myself by indulging in brandy the night I asked my wife's father for her hand in marriage, I decided then for the remainder of my days that it must be temperance for me if not total sobriety." He began to gather up a number of small sacks of seeds that James had prepared and laid on the counter.

Turning back to give Luke a hand, and especially regarding a large sack of seed corn sitting on the floor and slinging it over his shoulder, James said, "But you're a long time away from that night, Luke, and a big drink of good whiskey could give you a brace against that weather out there."

"No doubt, James, but I'd better not. And you're right about that night so long ago, I'm a long time away from it, a very long time." Luke said.

James placed the large sack of seed corn on the floor of the buggy while Luke placed the small sacks of seed on the buggy seat beside him. Then they turned and shook hands with James Mallory wishing Luke the best and Godspeed. And as the store owner stood and watched the buggy pull away from his store as he had done many times over the years, he was hard put on this day to understand his feelings. He felt that something was dreadfully wrong with the whole scene.

And now, as much as Luke was grateful that he was finally covering the sleet-coated drive at Green Sea and would not have to wonder any longer if he were going to hold out to reach home or not, he was more thankful to be there because of his horse – thankful and relieved, too, to know that the horse would soon be out of the cold, pouring sleet and safe in its stall. Still, having become sicker and wearier by the minute, it seemed since leaving Georgetown, Luke was not too certain about anything anymore and could not help wondering if he was truly hearing a voice calling to him, or was having hallucinations. But, suddenly, becoming aware that someone was running beside the buggy and calling to him, he peered through the sleet and recognizing the face of his son, his whereabouts and his thoughts were no longer a question with him.

Promptly bringing the buggy to a stop, Luke said, trying to force a lightness he did not feel, "Sorry about the chase, son, I gather you're out here to see if I had made it back yet or not. Some weather we're having. Jump in and we'll try to make it on to the barn."

"Yes, Papa, Mother's so worried about you, I was just starting to the barn to get my horse to go look for you when I saw you turn in from the road. You get out and go on inside to the fire. I'll take the buggy and the seeds you purchased on to the barn and see about your horse." Carr leaned forward, peering more closely into his father's face. "Papa, what's wrong? You look as though you're feeling something terrible. Are you sick?"

"Well, I'm not feeling my best, son, that's for sure. I've been chilling on and off since around noon, and feeling feverish to boot. I can't wait to get indoors and fall in bed. Nothing to worry yourself about though. It's probably just the grippe." Keeping the pain he was also suffering from to himself, he slowly got from the buggy and, handing the horse's reins to Carr, he went on, "Here, I'm thankful to turn these over to you and let you take care of things. Thanks, son."

"You bet, Papa, and you hurry on inside and don't worry about a thing. I'll take care of it." Carr said, thinking to himself as he mouthed the remarks the grippe was something to be much concerned about. Sometimes, it killed its victim! Suddenly, as Carr jumped inside the buggy to drive it on to the barn, he became gripped with a cold chill too. However, Carr felt assured that his chill was not bred from anything but mortal fear.

From the moment that Luke came through the kitchen door

and partly stumbled into Eliza's arms, until a little less than thirty-six hours later, the battle was on to save his life. And nobody fought any harder or more fiercely than Eliza, and all the while she fought, she was wishing over and over again that if it was the grippe that Luke was suffering from – something he believed himself – instead of the double-pneumonia that Doctor Seth Roalf diagnosed and gravely pronounced to her later on in the evening of that same day.

No sooner than Eliza had set her eyes on Luke, she had known that he was seriously ill and began to do everything and anything that one could do to turn his physical condition for the better. In double-quick time she had Luke out of his clothes and tucked between warm blankets in bed. Then, dashing back to the kitchen where she would be out of earshot of Luke – she knew he would worry as well as disapprove if he knew she was sending Carr to Elms in the sleet storm – she asked Phil Carson to hurry to the barn and tell Carr to take the closed carriage and go after Doctor Seth as quickly as he could possibly make it – a bidding that Phil did not only do on the instant as he saw the fear in Eliza's eyes, but he also volunteered to accompany Carr to Elms as well.

In the meantime, while she awaited Doctor Seth Roalf's arrival, Eliza dashed back and forth between the bedroom and the kitchen applying every home remedy that she had ever heard of such as hot broths, herb teas, and the usual onion and mustard poultices in hopes of bring some degree of improvement to the obvious pain, fever, and chills Luke was suffering from. Still, although she knew Luke was fighting as hard not to give in to his sickness as she was trying to bring some relief to him, it was obvious that no matter what she had done or was doing that not one thing had helped him. For he was growing worse by the hour. All she had to do to know was to lay her hand on his brow. His fever was climbing higher and higher and as it did, it weighed on her heavier and heavier.

Beginning to feel so weighed down that she would not have been surprised had she discovered the clothes she were wearing was made of wood, she stepped to the window and pulled back the curtains once again, anxiously looking down the drive for the carriage on its return from Elms despite her knowing she was not going to see it because Carr and Phil had not had time to return yet. However, as she peered through the window this time, she did see something that gave her an unexpected degree of lightness of body for it was snowing, big feather-like flakes that already had the outside grounds looking like a white frosted cake!

Thinking back to another time that it snowed and she and Luke had played in it like two frisky puppies, she stepped back to his bedside and said, "Luke, it's snowing, looking for all the world out there like someone might have taken the notion to turn a goose featherbed inside out. It's so pretty. How I wish it was morning instead of near nightfall, and you were well and you and I could go outside and enjoy it together for as long as it lasts, take a long walk in it and feel the snowflakes blowing against our faces."

"I wish we could too, Love, since it is so pretty and it visits us so seldom," Luke murmured, trying to send her a smile through his fever-glazed gaze. "Still, we must remember that most things balance out and the seasons are no excep – tion." A fit of coughing had broken his last word. Then, after a sip of water that Eliza had readily put to his lips, he went on, making all effort to talk, "Remember last June and our trip to the glade, the love we shared in all that beauty and the things we talked about there? That's what I mean by saying things usually balance out. In fact, no one season, no one circumstance, or anything else we meet with, no matter how pleasurable to us should ever be viewed as being the ultimate in giving us happiness. Try to remember that always and the things we talked about that day."

All of a sudden, feeling no colder than had she been standing in the snowy weather outside without one stitch of clothing on, Eliza was more than wise to what Luke had tried to tell her without coming right out and saying it, telling her he may not recover, and his wish was that she accept it!

Falling to her knees beside his bed and burying her head in

the bedcovers close to his, she moaned in disbelief, "Luke, you must get well. I'm not used to your being sick like this. I feel so useless and helpless. I'd give all the world if it were mine to give to change places with you. I –"

"Shh – shh –," Luke weakly interrupted, running his fevered hand through her hair, "you mustn't let my illness burden you so. Besides, if it were you instead of me, think of all the stress I'd be under trying to supervise this household and keep it running as smoothly as you do. You wouldn't want such a burden as that put on me, would you?" He let his hand fall from her hair to find hers, which she had clenched together and resting on the bedcovers, and gave them a little squeeze.

"N – o – o," she choked, despite the depth of her anguish. "I've never wanted anything for you, Luke, but your happiness and well-being. But, no matter how hard I've prayed and yearned for it to be that way for you, all too often, it's been quite the contrary as you well know." A faint sound of spinning carriage wheels was suddenly bringing her head upright and whirling her thoughts in another direction with her, adding, "I think I hear a carriage coming."

Still trying to spare her the gravity of his condition, Luke, forcing another weak smile, said, "Our carriage, Love, the one you sent to Elms to fetch Seth. I might've known."

His forced lightness made it easy for Eliza to look beyond her despair and smile back at him as she said, "And I might've known that you've been on to what I've been watching for from the window all along. But, let me see for sure." She jumped to her feet and, racing back to the window, she was readily going on – exclaiming in excitement – "He came, Luke, Seth's here! He's jumping from the carriage now and making for the front door!" She whirled around and headed for the bedroom doorway. "I'm going to run and meet him! Seth's going to have you back on your feet in no time, Luke, you'll see!" And with Luke's faint smile upon her still and following her, she went sailing on from the bedroom to greet Seth Roalf and usher him to Luke's bedside – her feet flying over the floorboards with a lightness that she was not to move with again for a long time to come. For, all too quickly, their long-time friend and family physician was turning away from his examination of Luke and, indiscreetly, giving her the nod to follow him as he was leaving the bedroom to go to the kitchen to mix a number of drugs with water to treat Luke with. Though the doctor deeply feared that the medicine he was going to prepare and give to Luke was going to fall way short in bringing the malady the latter was suffering from under control despite all the success he had had before with it.

"What is it, Seth?" Eliza asked, in a voice near trembling with fear no sooner than they had closed the bedroom door and were alone in the hallway. "What do you want me to know that you prefer Luke doesn't know?"

With an expression hanging heavy as lead, or nearabout, the doctor said, "It isn't that I prefer to keep what I have to say from Luke, Eliza. It's just that I think it's best that I discuss his condition with you out of his presence. Luke's a very sick man, Eliza, more serious I fear than even he himself realizes despite all the pain and misery he does feel. You see, dear, Luke doesn't have the grippe. His illness is far worse than that. He's suffering from double pneumonia and it's bad. The congestion is in both lungs, and it's my belief the pneumonia bacteria has been in his system for quite some time, even days perhaps. Anyway, it's an advanced case. That's one reason you haven't been able to get his fever to fall in spite of everything you've already done in order to make it fall. I deeply regret that I cannot say that it is the grippe and spare you the burden of knowing the seriousness of his condition, spare you of being aware of what the odds are of pulling him through. I feel for the sake of your own well-being that you should know how serious he is and try to prepare yourself not to be too optimistic. Still, we're going to keep trying, Eliza, you and me. We're going to keep fighting that fever with –"

All at once, seeing that all blood was draining from Eliza's face, to say nothing of her eyes taking on a look of horrifying terror, Seth Roalf was suspending his remarks and saying instead, as he made a grab for Eliza's arm, "What is it, Eliza?

Here, maybe it might be best you take this chair." He started to help her over to the side chair beside the wall that he had indicated she take but felt her resisting to move from the spot she stood in.

Giving Eliza a closer scrutiny and coming to the conclusion that she appeared to be more frozen in her tracks than she was reluctant to leave them, actually paralyzed by some frightful object that her gaze was fastened on. So, trying to reach her again and break the terrible trance she appeared to be in, the doctor said, "I'm terribly sorry, Eliza, I didn't mean to suggest that Luke's case is hopeless. I'd say he has an even chance and that's a lot more to look forward to and work toward than if there were no chance at all. We must think in those terms and have faith and not give up. But, for now, dear, I want you to take this chair and rest for a few minutes while I go on to the kitchen and prepare his medicine."

Once again, however, as the doctor gestured for Eliza to take the chair and rest a spell, he saw that not only did her feet appear to be glued to the floor she was standing on, but she was not hearing one word that he was saying as her fixed gaze continued to stare vacantly into space.

Wondering what to do or say next, in fact, the doctor was rapidly giving thought to maybe a hard slap was what it was going to take to bring Eliza out of her trance-like state, he decided to ask her pointblank if she were alright even though he was aware his question was going to sound stupid. Because it was obvious, she was far from being alright.

All the same, Doctor Seth Roalf, heard himself ask, "Eliza, are you alright? For heaven's sake, tell me what's wrong!" Then, with the pressure of desperation pushing him further, he added, "What are you looking at? What do you see that I don't?"

He anxiously waited for some response, feeling while he waited that he was walking on a tightrope.

Finally, after some little while and well-timed at that, because the doctor was bringing his hand up, out of his desperation, to give Eliza a slap in order to bring her out of the hypnotic state she appeared to be immersed in, Eliza said, proving she had heard every word the doctor had said. "No, I'm not all right, Seth, nor will I truly ever be again. Luke's in his death bed, Seth, he's going to die!"

Her self-control and obvious resignation were no less staggering to Seth Roalf, than her out of the blue prediction.

Aghast, but trying to keep his voice down, the doctor exclaimed, "Good Lord, Eliza, whatever made you say that? Apparently, you're so worried and not thinking straight, that you've misunderstood everything I've said. Here, I'm going to insist that you take this chair, and at least sit in it for the length of time it takes me to go to the kitchen to prepare his medicine."

"No, Seth," she promptly declared, brushing the doctor's hand off her arm and turning back toward the bedroom door. "I'm going back and spend every minute that I can with Luke." Let Seth and everybody else think what they would, she was thinking. There was no explaining her feelings to anybody, to say nothing of the shocking experience that she had just undergone. In fact, she very likely had already voiced too much as it was. And yet, all things considered, it was amazing to her that she was as rational as she was and not screaming her head off, screaming because she had just sighted the most shocking vision that had ever appeared before her eyes! Certainly, it was not an easy thing to undergo to see a vision of yourself kneeling down over a newly, flower-banked grave that had every living family member gathered around it and you, except your husband who was gravely ill at the time! No, she would never try to explain to Seth or anyone else that sometimes she knew beforehand what was to come. This was one thing she had never told to anyone, not even Luke, for fear of people looking on her as being crazy, or worse still, of being a witch! She had come to believe long years back that it was a gift from God, and she would hold it in secret between Him and herself. For on occasion, its power had given her deep joy and peace of mind when she was greatly troubled. Then again, it had also rendered her the worst kind of pain and heartache like moments ago. And yet, another possibility regarding the scene that she had just seen, that had nearly paralyzed her, could be God's way of preparing her for the inevitable, bad or good. Then again, with Seth informing her that Luke was suffering from the dread pneumonia and in both lungs at that, as well as her ever intense fear of the disease, could have caused her imagination to run wild and she had imagined the horrible scene only in her mind. Yes, she must hold to thinking that nothing had appeared before her eyes and try not to give in to the dread and fear that weighed on her. She must steel her feelings and be strong. No, not for herself, but be as strong and brave as she could possibly be for Luke. And above all, she must hold to her resolve not let it cave in and show in her manner as well!

Thus, swallowing the sobs that were lodged in her throat and taking a deep breath against the cold shudder that cut through her, Eliza Heyward reached for the doorknob that gained entrance into the bedroom where Luke was and gave it a turn. And having kept his eyes on Eliza's back until he saw her disappear through the bedroom doorway, Doctor Seth Roalf, shaking his head from side to side, turned and went on down the hall toward the kitchen.

The falling winter twilight turned to night and as the dark gathered and fell over the land, obscuring the light of day upon the snow-covered landscape and seeping throughout the mansion at Green Sea like a creeping black shroud and also engulfing Eliza in its somberness as well. Her whole being felt as though some mighty rolling stone had smashed into her and left nothing but the awful pain in her heart. For as the hours of night ticked away toward another dawn, and no matter how hard she and the doctor struggled to change Luke's condition for the better, not the tiniest improvement could they detect. Indeed, had there been some change for the better, Eliza would have been the first person to discover it. Because, true to her determination, she had not left Luke's bedside, nor once. She was there to hold the different glasses of medicine to his lips. Her hands were the hands that bathed his burning brow. It was her hands that kept the bedcovers tucked around him, and finally, it was her hand that clasped one of his hands and held onto it as steadfast as iron cast in cement.

Hour by hour, Eliza sat holding onto Luke's hand and silently praying that he would pull through despite the odds against it. Doctor Seth Roalf continued to labor on, too, with all the medical knowledge he possessed, but fearing he was leaving something undone for Luke that should be done, he suggested that Doctor Cyrus Vance, the former Grace Cooper's husband, who was noted to have specialized in respiratory diseases be summoned to Luke's bedside. Doctor Seth Roalf Junior and his wife Maggie also came to give what assistance they could. But, despite anything that all three doctors did or anything else that was applied relative to one fighting the dread pneumonia, nothing changed for the better.

Pete prepared supper and even though Eliza did insist that everybody march on to the dining room and eat, she herself refused to join them or eat one bite from the tray that Pete prepared and took to the bedroom for her. In fact, she bypassed all nourishment in any form, food and drink as well. She did nothing but keep to her vigil at Luke's bedside, watching and observing his every move as well as keeping on the alert to grasp and respond to the few faint words that he continued to whisper to her. Though by this hour, Luke's remarks of love to her and those of his trying to reassure her in point of his recovery were becoming fewer and wider apart and growing more so by the hour.

Then as the long hours of that night slipped into the breaking of another day, all whispers from Luke slipped with it, snuffed out by the deep-fevered oblivion which he had fallen in and which Eliza and Doctor Seth Roalf had feared and fought so desperately against. And yet, even though Luke's condition had become more critical, silencing his words and taking his mind and thoughts from all goings on and everybody around him, never once did Eliza entertain the thought of giving up her watch and leaving his bedside. She was determined to remain where she was, her drawn face revealing a kind of suffering that it had never worn before – a different agony and heartache that made her feel as though a knife was being inched into her heart upon the sound of every shallow breath that fell from Luke in the death-like silence around her. Indeed, when it came to one's appearance – whose face looked less drawn, Luke's or Eliza's? Luke would have won hands down! As a matter of fact, at this point in Luke's illness, he appeared to have escaped from all pain, looking to be in a deep sleep more than anything else. In brief, it was Eliza Heyward in her awareness who was suffering now, enduring the most painful anguish that she had ever experienced as she continued to watch Luke slipping away from her with every breath he took and wondering if it would be the last breath he took.

The light of day brought a landscape looking as a whole as though it might have turned into a white flower blossom overnight! Everything was blanketed in a heavy coat of white, a breathtaking and delightful kind of dress that one seldom saw the region clothed in. Still, when it came to Luke Heyward's family and friends taking any delight from the snow-blanketed land, or in most cases even seeing it, a briar patch would have caught their attention and thrilled them no less! And, this indifference regarding the weather was especially true to those who had been informed about Luke and found themselves in the cold of their carriages headed toward Green Sea the next morning. Two in particular were Bruce and Martha Randolph.

"I just can't believe it's only a matter of hours with him," Bruce solemnly declared, gazing at the snow and not even seeing it, because his mind's eye was too fixed upon the mental pictures crowding his head, scenes of his and Luke's numerous past business dealings and the many interests they shared and enjoyed together. "Luke's never been sick a day in his life that I know of."

For once, the first time in her life as a matter of fact, Martha turned her head to comment on Bruce's remarks and found herself in scant supply of words – if any! Granted, the news that Luke was dying had floored her too, and seeing the pain and grief on Bruce's face had thwarted her desire to try to lighten the message that had planted it there that much more.

So, sorrow-stricken herself as well as feeling that she had let Bruce down by not saying one word to him in his sorrow over Luke, Martha turned her head back to the carriage window and fixing her unattentive gaze upon the snow again silently aired her despair to her ears alone, telling herself that the words she so desperately wanted to phrase to Bruce were out of the question anyway. There simply was no way to say that everything was going to be alright when the circumstances of their going to Green Sea were so unexpected and out of keeping from the usual run of things, not to mention that some things were never going to be the same again! No way to say that the great void of Luke's presence was not going to be in their lives to Bruce, because be there it would and very painful at that. No way to try to smooth over the fact that the pattern of his and Luke's relationship of seeing one another on an average of two or three times a week due to business dealings, or simply to enjoy their many interests together would not end for all time. For death unlike most any aspect of life is so final, it's as permanent and immovable as the universe itself. And for one to think or talk otherwise in order to try to comfort one's grief would not only sound senseless but be senseless, to her way of thinking Martha told herself. And worse still, what on earth was she going to say to Eliza when they came face to face with one another. She could hardly bear to give thought to that another second!

All at once, with the thought of facing Eliza as well as the grievous circumstances of everything else overwhelmed Martha so that she finally gave way to the cramps that were squeezing her throat and let her tears wash as they would. Then just as quickly with her overstrung nature kindling a flame of anger in her at the unfairness of the whole matter – or what Martha deemed as being unfair – she was reaching for Bruce's hand and telling herself that she must not become a softy, no gingerbread because too many people were going to be counting on her to hold up and comfort them instead of the other way around! For in addition to Eliza and Bruce, Luke Heyward's two children and his three grandchildren were going to need her support and comfort too.

Martha Randolph tightened her grip on her husband's hand.

Over the snow-packed and crusty ruts the carriage rolled on with Martha observing as it entered the long drive at Green Sea and rolled on toward the mansion's front steps and stopped, that aside from the vast difference in the weather, the entire scene reminded her of that long ago day when Frank was lying on his deathbed at Drakston Hall. Carriages and buggies were parked everywhere. It appeared that in spite of the unfavorable weather conditions, not only had the terrible news spread far and wide, but the weather had also been of no concern whatever in keeping those who had heard about it away. All the same, Martha was not so simple that she did not realize that no one person had come to Green Sea on this day for the mere sake of curiosity alone as it had been with the majority of those of who had heard about Frank and had flocked to Drakston Hall. These people had braved snow-packed roads to come to Green Sea for one reason and only one reason at that, and that was because of their high esteem for Luke Heyward. Martha was certain of that!

At all events, and all too soon at that for Martha, Martha was presently inside the mansion and its dismal atmosphere, solemnly nodding to several acquaintances whom she recognized – mostly fellow members of the local Baptist church as she and Bruce made their way down the hall and into the bedroom where Luke was barely clinging to life, with Martha noting the instant her eyes fell upon Eliza that she was certain the latter had fallen into a stunned and unknowing state of not even being aware of where she was, or anything or anybody around her as she sat beside Luke's bed gripping one of his hands. Indeed, Martha had summed up the whole of Eliza's emotions as thoroughly as had she been a noted intellectual of the mind! And, Martha's theory was brought to light as clearly as a bell ringing a few short hours later.

Martha also noted that a number of family members and friends were gathered in the room as well. Doctor Seth Roalf Senior, looking like he might topple upon the bed himself from exhaustion, was standing on the same side of the bed where Eliza sat and as close to her chair as possible. Phil Carson was stationed on the other side of the bed opposite him. Phil hardly looked any more rested and less haggard than this long-time family doctor did. Brent Cooper, Martha noted, apparently having just arrived and entering the bedroom before she and Bruce did, because he was still wearing his hat and coat having taken no time to shed either, was off to one side of the bedroom conferring with his son-in-law Doctor Cyrus Vance in a muffled voice, with the doctor slowly shaking his head from side to side. The younger Doctor Seth Roalf and his wife Maggie were also in attendance. And, of course, both of Luke Heyward's children were there. Jane Anne, with Stuart seated beside her and holding her hand along with his arm draped around her shoulders, had her head buried in the palms of her hands as she continued to quietly grieve for her beloved Papa.

Carr Heyward, who was standing on the other side of his mother's chair, upon seeing Martha come through the doorway, turned and placing a chair in the spot he had been occupying indicated to Martha to take it. Martha, silently respecting Carr's wishes, stepped on toward the bed and quietly settling herself down in the chair draped an arm around Eliza's shoulders even though she was positive that Eliza was unaware of her presence, or gesture of sympathy either. Martha was too full of sadness to trust her voice to speak to Eliza. So, she remained silent as likewise to Bruce who had silently and solemnly planted himself at the foot of the huge four poster that Luke lay upon without speaking to Eliza or anybody else as he kept his gaze fixed solidly on Luke's face. All in all, Martha Randolph felt it was one of the most distressing situations she had ever found herself in, if not the worst!

At all events, perhaps no longer than two hours later, the whole desolate scene stayed pretty much the same with nothing of significance taking place to alter it, or change with those who had gathered in the bedroom waiting – waiting in a painful hush with only the faint ebbing sound of Luke's breath becoming shorter and shorter. Then, almost to the same time of day at near the hour of eleven o'clock that morning, when Luke had walked into Eliza's life, he was to take a last breath and slip peacefully out of it. And most assuredly, Eliza still remained at Luke's bedside, her stunned gaze never leaving his face. Nor did she appear to have moved a muscle as well as giving every sign she was not going to and remain in her same stationary position indefinitely as she continued to hold onto Luke's hand with a steadfast grip.

And so, Seth Roalf Senior also sizing up the state of Eliza's emotions no less as Martha had, as well as deeply deploring the move he saw he must make, reached down and as gently as he possibly could, unlocked her hand from Luke's and said, "Eliza, dear, there's nothing more we can do but give him to God. You must come with me."

Then, like a shot, there was nothing but action with Eliza Heyward and frenzied action at that. To everybody's apprehension and intense shock as well – aside from Martha Randolph – Eliza instantly brushed the doctor's hand aside and jumped to her feet in a run, moving as though she might have been a deer in flight. She belted through the doorway, fleeing as fast as her feet could move from the unbelievable nightmare that she was positive she was undergoing, running as fast as she had ever moved in her entire life on down the hallway and down the stairs and through the front door and on across the porch and down the steps into the snowy grounds! She continued to run, headed straight for the river road even though she was unaware of where she was, leaving startled callers behind her and also lost in wonder as to what she would do next and Doctor Seth Roalf Senior and her son Carr Heyward in dumbfounded pursuit of her to boot! She ran on in the blistery outdoors and was almost to the river road when she ran headlong into a low snow-laden limb from one of the live oaks and fell face down into its snowy deep foliage.

Although the fall stunned Eliza and she was crying herself blind as well, she never paused in her effort to awaken and escape from the unreal trauma of the nightmare she had fantasized in her mind rather than face the reality of her intense grief. That is, until the heavy, icy live oak branches began to pinch and sting her fingers and hands and the penetrating pain abruptly made her aware of where she was instead of lying beside Luke in the featherbed they shared, trying to run from the phantom chasing her! And then, if there was one fraction of doubt lingering in her mind that the dread pneumonia had taken Luke from her forever, the frantic voice of her son calling to her was the final blow of reality as he fell down beside her and cried, "Oh, Mother, please don't leave us too! If we've ever needed your strength and support, we need it now! Here, let Uncle Seth and me help you back to the house!"

He reached for one of her hands that was clutching a fistful of icy live oak leaves. With tears streaming down her face and feeling as though a knife had sliced her in half, Eliza, realizing she must try to do what her son was asking of her, lifted her hand to meet the hand of her son and with him and the doctor on either side of her, she slowly covered the snow-packed grounds back to the house. And, added to the agony of her grief, Eliza had told herself with every reluctant step she had taken that the house that had given Luke and herself so much pleasure and joy was never going to do the same to her again, no matter how many footsteps it might support or how much laughter may fall in its rooms in the future ahead.

Although Green Sea had seen and withstood the demise of one of its own before the passing away of Luke Heyward, his death seemed to be different and set apart from those deaths having occurred there before him. Perhaps it was owing to Luke's high moral decency, or maybe because of his known good deeds relative to his family, his community and his fellow man. Then again, perhaps it was due to Luke having been the unmoneyed outsider who had come to the Lowcountry and, right off, had fit in so splendidly with its rich as well as its poor and penniless, to say nothing of Lowcountry tradition and customs too.

In any case, one could not dispute a difference did exist in regard to Luke Heyward's death. For not only was it obvious that the news of his death had hit people with a greater impact

– in most cases having brought instant tears of grief – but it also brought a number of folk to want to do more than just grieve for him, namely the two sharecroppers, Willie and Allen, who took it upon themselves to dig the grave, because they wanted to see that the job was done right so they had remarked to Phil Carson when they had approached him about the matter. In addition, both Bruce Randolph and Bill Cooper were moved to pay verbal tribute to Luke's honorable character and many worthy deeds at the funeral – a first time thing for both men to do but felt compelled to carry through with it. Of course, Reverend Marsh Reed preached the funeral, bellowing too loud and too long, Eliza was thinking throughout the ordeal of bearing with it. And yet, had she been of a mind to let the Reverend on to her thoughts, she would not have been able to carry through with it because, by this time, she had mourned and cried so much she had rendered herself beyond even managing to whisper a word! All she could manage in the way of acknowledging people's sympathy was to bob her head somewhat or lightly squeeze their hand. She was unable to mouth one word to Tom and Betsy Green or Gilford and Lucy Sloan when they had spoken to her no matter how hard she made an effort to, knowing their deep devotion for Luke. Yes, Phil Carson had wired both Tom Green and Gilford Sloan that Luke was seriously ill and not expected to live, and both men, along with their wives, made haste for Green Sea and did arrive in time for the funeral.

Still, talk or no talk, Eliza was determined to stay on her feet and follow Luke's remains as far and long as it was possible to do even if the endeavor came to be the last of her, which if it had come to that, would not have surprised anybody considering how haggard and grieved she looked. However, more for the sake of her two children than herself, Eliza continued to strive with all the strength she was capable of to keep believing that Luke was indeed gone and was not going to be with her any more. But, even so, she found herself, involuntarily, looking for him and searching for his face among the mourners even at the gravesite in spite of the harsh evidence of his death and his burial right before her eyes, to say nothing of hearing Marsh Reed repeating the lines of the old proverb in the book of Ecclesiastes, "to everything there is a season and a time to every purpose under the heaven," and yes, as it had been with her mother, it was a favorite of Luke's too. In brief, it was going to take time and apparently a lot of time at that for Eliza to execute a full fadeout of Luke and refrain from separating him from the burial service altogether and place him among the living again!

Be as it may; however, it happened to be a combination of two things that finally gave Eliza the ability to accept the real truth from the unreal and at the precise moment when she had needed it most besides. First, it was her deep abiding faith in God and His teachings and especially His word that death was not the ending of a Believer's life but the beginning of their afterlife. The second, to Eliza's thinking was a spiritual happening. For when it came time for Luke's coffin to be lowered to its final resting place – a time that Eliza had dreaded most and the one thing she had doubted she could stand up to – she found her faith buoying her on beyond any hope she had ever imagined when suddenly the clouds above were giving way to let a brilliant stream of sunlight pour down on the coffin, shrouding it like a warm blanket and moving Eliza to feel as though God had opened His arms and gathered Luke in the warmth of His love. So overwhelmed at the sun's rays reflecting on the metal coffin like a cloth of gold unlike it no longer was within her sight gave Eliza the strength to turn away and feel she was not leaving Luke in the cold of death after all, but in the joy of living on as she made her way in hesitant steps back to the mansion that she and Luke had struggled so long and so hard together to build.

Granted, it went without saying that, following Luke's death, Eliza's daily existence came to be totally empty. She did do what she felt was her duty to do like receiving visitors and seeing to the needs of her family and those of her household. But other than the time it took for these activities, the majority of her waking hours were spent in the cemetery, either sitting silently beside Luke's grave lost in her memories of him, or up on her feed digging furiously with her hoe as she worked at setting out flower plants and shrubs around it. Her behavior was no surprise to her family or anybody else though who knew her and was aware of her deep love and devotion for her husband. The fact was, they were expecting her to act no different and would have been more concerned than had she paid less visits to Luke's grave as well as less in length and frequency too. However, when weeks began to stretch into months and Eliza was still spending more time in the cemetery during the daylight hours than she spent at the house, these same family members and friends not only began to be much concerned about her but began to wonder if her habit of going to the cemetery and spending so much time there was going to be a permanent routine with her! In short, there seemed to be no healing for Eliza's grief. And, what's more, nobody was more aware of what Eliza's daily living pattern had become than Eliza herself! Certainly, she was fully aware that by spending so much time at Luke's grave she was chancing never gaining the strength and will she needed to pull herself up out of that dark well of grief that she had fallen into. And yet, by some inner force, she felt pulled in the worst way to be there. Feeling compelled to be no place else but where she was, hour upon hour she either sat dispiritedly on the base of Luke's headstone trying to come to some degree of understanding the grievous turn her life had taken, or up puttering with her hoe around his grave.

To Eliza Heyward, it made no sense at all that she and Luke were sitting at the breakfast table discussing spring planting one morning and before two more mornings fell, he was dead! Just like that! No lingering illness. No freak accident like a tree falling and smashing the life out of him. No becoming impaired by old age and fading away. Only a common sniffle or two and he was already on his way to his grave! One day her strong and vital husband. The next day dying and not one thing anybody could do to prevent it. No, to understand something like that was way beyond all the mental power she possessed, to say nothing of any measure of faith she had come by in her lifetime, Eliza told herself.

Eliza had held on to thinking that with the opening of spring, the shadows of grief that had darkened her days for so long would give a little and be lighter. But, from the opening of the first crocuses to the fading of the last buttercup, no light had come to make the pathways her feet trod upon any brighter. Her grief had obliterated it all, turning the bloom of spring into an empty vacuum. The one single thing that seemed to give one degree of calm to her grief was a letter that Luke had penned a few years back and had instructed his attorney, Bill Cooper, to hand to her upon his death and the reading of his will. She kept the letter tucked into her apron pocket so she could easily reach for it, something she did rather often.

And now, seated upon the base of Luke's headstone for still another time, Eliza drew the letter forth once more and began to read.

My Dearest Eliza,

Darling, since it appears to be a clear and unmistakable fact that time has a way of counting the years faster and faster as one begins to grow older and, particularly, once one comes to that stretch of years that are generally referred to as the decline of life, which I reached long back and which I have already covered a good portion of, I feel that penning this letter to you should not be put off any longer.

Yes, although sometimes when I look at you it is difficult for me to realize that there has been any time at all since that day at Windsor when I first saw you, I must not forget that the years have indeed fallen, and it is time for me to get on with seeing to the business of this letter. I will ask Bill Cooper to file it away along with my will and instruct him upon my death and after the reading of my will to hand it to you. Certainly, since I am a near decade the older of the two of us, it is reasonable to presume that in all probability I will proceed you in death – a presumption that I assure you I feel comfortable with and the way I truly prefer it to be – because I cannot any more contemplate life without you than I can think about the sun and the moon never shedding light upon this earth again.

At any rate, I am trusting that my decision to name Whitney Randolph Carson in my will as my legal heir to the rights that I held and control regarding Green Sea's vast lands and cultivated acreage – rights that your father so generously bequeathed to me – will not only meet with your approval, but Phil's as well. I believe that it will, for I pondered over this matter a great deal and finally concluded that it was the principled thing to do. You see, since it appears to have been the will of God that He bring our only son and Phil's only child and daughter together and make them husband and wife, as well as taking into account that our son will eventually inherit the other one-half part of Green Sea that you hold, I feel this act on my part will more or less render everything fair and just among those of whom who are indeed the legitimate and rightful heirs to Green Sea. There is no question that your late brother Nat is Whit's father. Although the subject was never opened and discussed between your late father and me just as you and I both have ever chosen not to discuss it even to the question of when and how your father became aware of the matter and up and readily gave Whit his legal name by adopting him!

So, seeing the matter as being something that not only is resting with me and should be done, but also something that your father would certainly approve of if he were here, I shall do my duty and will Whit his birthright, a birthright that within a few years he may claim. For Stuart tells me that Whit has written to him that he could be calling the Navy quits and coming back to these parts sooner than he previously thought. It sounds as though Whit's hunger to sail the world's oceans and explore all those exotic parts he sails into has been quenched somewhat. In any case, and whatever his final decision is, his birthright is now set to rights for him.

Of course, Sweetheart, I will all my personal effects to you. My bank stock and bonds, as well as all the legal tender I hold in silver, gold and folding money to use and dispose of as you see fit. Moreover, the mansion and all its contents, as well as its surrounding grounds and outer buildings and all other structures will be solely yours to control as you see fit to do.

I suppose this just about covers all the business matters I wanted to clarify in case any questions are raised in point of my will after I am gone. As far as the feelings I hold in my heart, I want you to know that a happier life than I have experienced with you, I have never visioned or harbored for one fraction of a second. Granted, there have been a number of bad times along with all the good years we have seen together. But even those bad periods, which we did wade through and which we find ourselves no worse off for, in my book so to speak, were better than no years would have been. Thus, let us trust that all the love and devotion we have for one another and have shared in this present world, we may come to know and share still in the next to come.

All My Love Forevermore,
Luke

Letting her gaze rest on the last words that Luke had penned to her, Eliza became aware that a most surprising thing had taken place with her! She could finally read the letter and get through it without having to stop and wipe at her tears every few lines. Moreover, and as surprising and curious as this was to her too, the soothing effect that the letter had always brought to her with every tearful reading was no longer there. Instead, not only did she find herself feeling more down than ever, but she also had become aware she was harboring quite a degree of anger too, and to make it worse, she did not know whom she was angry with or why she was angry! All she was certain of was the angry feeling was there. Though she only gave herself a fraction of a second to even consider such a thing lest she was being disloyal to Luke's memory, she thought perhaps she had become angry with Luke for dying and leaving her to try to go on alone without him. Yes, even though she felt that it was monstrous of her to give rise to such a thought, she had to admit that somehow a blaze of anger had found its way into her grief for Luke and she was unable to account for it being there! She thought she had already suffered and endured every phase of grief known to man, and now a feeling of anger had surfaced from somewhere, and she did not have the least idea why it was there or how she was going to deal with it, if she ever did!

However, as Eliza continued to sit upon Luke's headstone, reflecting over this new and baffling emotion that had assailed her person and trying to find a reason for it being there, it abruptly came to her that whatever else it may do to her that some good had already come from it, in that, she had finally ceased her weeping! Yes, she was positive that in order for the tears to stop spilling down her face that it was inevitable that she felt a degree of anger as outlandish as it was!

Hearing the hinges on the gate to the cemetery give a sudden squeak, Eliza looked up and saw Martha entering the cemetery. Slipping the letter back inside her apron pocket, she gave a long, weary sigh and called, "Come on up here, Martha. I can't imagine why you chose to walk so far in the hot sun. You shouldn't have, you know."

"What about yourself?" Martha called back, plodding on up the hill toward Luke's grave. Then, taking the last step that lay between her and where Eliza was seated, she added, "Move on over and let me rest a spell. And I'll confess if I've been reluctant to think about my age here lately, that walk has sure brought it home to me!"

Responding to Martha's first remark as she let the one about age do a fast death, Eliza said, "But I came early. I didn't wait till the middle of the morning to walk up here."

"Yes, no doubt you did, and if you follow your usual pattern, the sun won't be any problem when you decide to leave," fired Martha. "Honest, Eliza, when are you going to stop spending so much time here? You've got to let Luke go. You know good and well that he'd be the first to tell you that very thing – tell you to get on with your life – well, what's left of it, anyway!"

The usual sermon, or near it, Eliza thought to herself as she turned and looked Martha straight in the face and repeated, her anger blaring in both her eyes as well as her voice, "Let him go! You haven't the least idea, Martha, what you're saying let along know anything about my feelings. You might as well tell me that my life with Luke never existed at all and that not only is it stupid of me to be grieving over something that never was, but insane as well!"

"No, Eliza, you know better than that and you've got it all wrong, but I'm not going to quarrel with you. Regardless of what you may think, feel or say, there are a great number of others who have and still are grieving for Luke too. Why, Bruce has grieved so that he actually has fallen ill a number of times – gone all to pieces and I've had to send for Seth and -- ."

"That's the first I've heard of that," Eliza suddenly interrupted. "Why didn't you tell me?"

"Because you've never bothered to ask once how he's doing, that's why! Besides, had I tried to tell you, I'm positive you wouldn't have heard me. To tell you the truth, Eliza, I think the only reason you're hearing me now is that you're angry about something. Yes, angry for a change instead of grieving!"

Taking her unsettled gaze away from Martha to look into the distance, Eliza said, "I didn't know it showed that much."

"Well, it does," affirmed Martha. "One would have to be blind and deaf too, not to know. Who are you angry with? What's happened?"

"Nothing's happened, that's what!" snapped Eliza. "That's just the point. It's always the same, a feeling of being lost, literally, day in and say out!" She refused to hold to her earlier thought and say she believed her deceased husband had something to do with her anger.

Puzzled, Martha questioned, measuring Eliza with a narrowed eye, "Lost? You mean you've become angry because you feel lost?"

"I suppose, yes, I guess it's something like that," Eliza said, the anger in her voice dissipating somewhat as she turned back to Martha and went on, "Does that make any sense to you? It's like waking up to find yourself in strange surroundings with no idea of how you got there or what direction you want to go in. Sounds crazy, I know, so don't tell anyone else."

With her own temper having plunged back to its normal ebb as Eliza's remarks had fallen between them, Martha said, "What we talk about, Eliza, will stay with us as it always has. But I think you're wrong to say you sound crazy because, considering how devoted you and Luke were to one another and how many years you were together, I should think nobody would expect your feelings to be one bit different than the way you've just described them. I know I don't."

"Being angry too?" Eliza pressed.

"Certainly," Martha declared, hesitating not one second. "Now why I'm positive it would make me mad as a hornet, even with Bruce, himself, if pneumonia or anything else were to just up and snatch him away from me like Luke was snatched away from you! Now don't ask me how I know that. I just know, that's all!"

Amazed that Martha, as usual, had untangled this whole complex matter so quickly, hitting on the very thing that she had suspected about herself but had refused to face and come right out and say it like Martha had! And feeling so much better to know that Martha saw not one thing out of the ordinary by what she had revealed about herself – actually like Martha had made her swallow a soothing tonic – she suddenly wanted to share Luke's letter with Martha saying, "Martha, I want to share a letter with you that Luke wrote to me and asked Bill Cooper to file it away with his will and upon his death to give it to me. It appears that somehow Luke knew he was going first!"

Eliza reached inside her apron pocket and handed the letter to an obviously surprised Martha.

Reading the letter with open interest and quite a bit of astonishment too, Martha finally lifting her head and giving a long sigh that sounded as though she had just emerged from under a ton of weight said, "Well, I'm glad to see that fact finally disclosed and spelled out in broad letters before I do my breathing out! Luke, bless his heart, came right out and did that very thing, did what no member in this entire family ever had the nerve to do before! I wonder why, Eliza? Even you and I have always beat around the bush about it. Instead of coming right out and saying that we knew who Whit's parents were, we both just looked at one another and let the subject drop!"

"I know," agreed Eliza. "But I also think it was because of Nat's tragic death and the way everything turned out. It was as if we were being disloyal to his memory to talk about it." Then as the fall of a long, silent moment began to grow even longer, Eliza went on to inquire of Martha, asking, "Has Aunt Amy mentioned hearing from Whit lately?"

"Not for several weeks now she hasn't. But when she heard last, Whit did mention that he had received a letter and a packet of legal documents from Bill Cooper. So, I should think he knows all about the part he plays in Luke's will by now."

"Yes, I imagine he does," muttered Eliza. "What's your feelings about it, Eliza?" Martha ventured to ask. "Had you known what Luke was up to would you have tried to change his mind?"

"No, I don't think so," said Eliza, without hesitating for one second. "Because, you see, Luke saw every aspect of life as being either right or wrong. So naming Whit his legal heir to Green Sea was the right thing to do. Besides, as he pointed out, it was also his belief that he was doing something that Father would have approved and given his consent to. And knowing Father as I did, I believe that way too. In any case, Whit is a Carson. I don't think there's one family member who would attempt to deny that. So, when he does leave the Navy, let him come home to Green Sea where he belongs. Phil and I both have agreed that Green Sea is certainly big enough to accommodate him along with our own, not to mention Matt or any other children that Carr and Beth Anne may be blessed with. To tell the truth, nothing's really changed that much. Carr, because, of course, is still heir to my half of the land as well as the mansion and all other personal property. The half of the land that Father deeded to Luke is what Luke saw as being right to go to Whit. What strange happenings! My own blood nephew happens to be my adopted step-brother too!"

"What about me?" Martha promptly blurted. "Not only is

Whit my husband's true-blue nephew, but he's also my blood second cousin as well as adopted step-brother! Some family connection, if you ask me!"

And as Martha let this last statement drop, it brought both their heads turning toward one another again to exchange a look that was somewhat diverted from the troubled look that they both had been wearing earlier.

As ironic as it was when this conversation about Whit between Eliza and Martha was taking place, the naval ship that Whit served on and was assigned to had already reached American waters and at the completion of its sea duty had docked in the coastal harbor of Norfolk, Virginia.

Normally, no sooner than his ship's anchor had settled on the bottom of some American port once again, Whit had gathered his gear, so to speak, and was headed straight home, which, of course, meant the Lowcountry plantation, Drakston Hall, where he had grown up and also gone to school under the tutorship of Lucy Randolph in Drakston Hall's private schoolroom. However, on this occasion upon reaching American soil again instead of heading for Drakston Hall, he headed straight for the residence of Gilford and Lucy Sloan in Lexington, Virginia. Actually, visiting the Sloan's was no strange thing for Whit to do since he had always kept in touch with his former teacher and friend Lucy Randolph, before as well as after her marriage to Gilford Sloan. But the happy expectation and eagerness that had ever been his to feel at seeing "Miss Lucy" again was absent this time. Instead, he was deeply disturbed, troubled and weighed down with questions as well as bewildered and had been ever since he had received a document of legal papers from Bill Cooper's law firm informing him that the late Luke Heyward had named him his legal heir to thousands of acres to Green Sea's lands! And, the upper and main question in his mind as to why Luke Heyward had named him his legal heir to come into this vast heritage when the latter had two children of his own, namely Carr Heyward and Jane Ann Drakston!

In addition, the matter of his adoption had begun to concern

Whit intensely, something that had never bothered him before, not since he had become aware of it and he and Stuart had cried and cried to learn they were not blood brothers. But, Mama Amy and Papa Matthew, too, had explained as to why and that was because the war had displaced or taken so many lives, his own parents among them. And having been brought up in the security of their love and devotion at Drakston Hall as a Carson, not to mention the close family ties to the Heyward's and Randolph's as well, had ever been satisfactory and comforting enough for him. But all those legal papers from Bill Cooper had changed everything with his mind whirling with dozens of questions and incidents past. For instance, like the other day when he was shaving and trimming the whiskers on his chin and began to wonder who he favored, it suddenly hit him the day he and Carr were looking at the family portraits that had finally found their place on the wall in the new mansion at Green Sea again after so many years and Carr had piped up and said, "Whit, if I didn't know better, I'd think that was you there with Mother and Uncle Phil. He was Nathan Carson, Mother's younger brother. He was killed at Yellow Tavern in sixty-four in the same battle that Jeb Stuart was mortally wounded." And he had agreed with Carr and they had laughed and he had thought no more about it. But not anymore. In fact, he had had not another thing on his mind since then. And recalling Carr's remarks about him looking like the late Nathan Carson, along with inheriting all that land at Green Sea from the late Luke Heyward in the latter's will had truly sent him whirling to the nearest chair in shock! Then in almost the next breath the shocking belief that doubtless Lucy Randolph Sloan was his real mother was crowding his mind! Yes, no doubt, he was the son of Nathan Carson and Lucy Randolph! For had not the love and devotion of Lucy Randolph for the long-deceased soldier who was killed at Yellow Tavern had ever been a subject to surface when discussing the war and its hardship and lasting change and effect on everything.

It had taken some little while for Whit Carson to gather his shock of reasoning and finally concluding he was indeed a

Carson and not some lost identity of the Civil War and get back to his personal grooming. All the same, no sooner than he thought he had absorbed the shock of knowing his true identity, he found himself taking on a great deal of anger as well as disappointment toward every family member whom he had ever known, old and young alike! Because he felt betrayed by each and every one, the Carson's, the Heyward's, and the Randolph's too! And, in point of Stuart Drakston and Carr Heyward, his feelings of being betrayed by them were much more intensified because of the closeness they had shared as playmates as well as when they had become grownups. Still, Whit's discovery about himself began to wear more lighter with time to think upon it, and he did come to see and understand a great deal of it in a different light. For one thing, he came to believe that his peers had heard or knew no more about his adoption than the story he himself was told, reasoning that Stuart and Carr would have blurted the secret out in their play at some point, and especially at some disagreement. Thus, he felt comforted by believing the younger family members were in the dark about his adoption too. However, there was the question of "Miss Lucy"? How did he feel about her? Well, after crowding his head for days – nights too – and weighing all aspects of the part of his adoption she had played, nothing had changed regarding his feelings toward her. If anything, he admired her more than ever, seeing her as being in an even more esteemed light than he had before. For because of her unselfish act and the personal sacrifice of her love for her baby, she had saved him from wearing the mark of a bastard – nobody's son – for his entire life! Yes, in his eyes, Miss Lucy, bore nothing but high character despite her all-possessing and tragic love for Nathan Carson.

Nevertheless, Whit Carson had no idea how he was going to react to Lucy Sloan's presence on this occasion, or for that matter, what he was going to say to her either. All he did know was by the time he found himself planted before the front door of the Sloan residence in Lexington and ready to sound the doorknocker, that all enduring esteem and close bond with

Lucy that had ever dwelled inside him was as afresh and rising as rapidly as it ever had in anticipation of seeing her.

And now as Lucy Sloan pulled on the doorknob and looked into Whit's face with astonishment – instantly noting that the sea's salt-driven winds had swept all youth from it as she tried to overcome her shock and find her voice while Whit was blithely laughing, "Don't faint, Miss Lucy, it's only me!" The "Miss Lucy" had fallen as easily from his lips as ever, with him to instantly realize that no matter what their talk may reveal during this visit or what surprise may fall, that to address her by any other name was simply inconceivable.

Pushing off her surprise and trying to give her voice the momentum it had lost, Lucy flashed back, "Well, it would serve you right if I did!" She stepped forth and threw both arms around him. Then drawing back, she went on, "But why didn't you let me know you were coming? I would've been more prepared, you know."

"Didn't exactly know myself, Miss Lucy, till I was already on my way. Our ship docked in Norfolk, so I thought since I was already in the state, I'd look you up before I went on home."

"It doesn't matter," she smiled. "All that matters is that you're here. Come on in." She motioned for him to precede her through the doorway, adding as she closed the door, "Sit any place you will, or would you like to come on into the kitchen while I put on a pot of coffee? You will take a cup, won't you?"

"The kitchen will be fine, Miss Lucy, and yes, so will the coffee."

With Whit sprawling himself into a chair at the kitchen table, Lucy asked, as she busied herself with putting the coffee on the stove and setting out a plate of cookies, "Where's your luggage, Whit? I haven't seen any."

"At the depot, Miss Lucy, I'll have to catch the night train out and be on my way."

"So soon?" she asked.

"I'm afraid so. Even then I won't get home till late

77

tomorrow some time. Although I do have a lot of business to take care of and a number of people to see when I do get there, I wanted to make sure that I also saw you and Mr. Gilford too. Mr. Gilford's doing all right, I trust?"

"Yes, Gilford's fine. He's down at the newspaper office, says gathering the news and seeing about that newspaper is good medicine that it keeps him from dwelling on his aches and pains and thinking about the fact that he isn't young anymore."

Whit laughed, "I suppose I would've been wise to have gone into the newspaper business then instead of joining the Navy like I did."

Pulling out a chair opposite him at the kitchen table and falling into it, Lucy said, as she sent him a wide smile, "Don't tell me you're worrying about growing old already? You're too young in years yet to bother your head with that, you know."

"No, not really, Miss Lucy, but there are a number of decisions I must make when I do get home that I'd prefer to put off for a while, or better still never have to make at all, if you know what I mean."

"Well, yes, I think I know. You're referring to Luke's will, the part you played in it when it was read and probated." Lucy said.

Surprised and relieved, too, that the subject of the will had opened so quickly and easily as well, Whit pressed, "So you've already heard about it?" He closely searched her face, trying to detect some clue to how she felt about the matter.

However, he quickly saw that any feeling she might hold or express, verbal or otherwise, had been briefly overpowered by a deep melancholy. He anxiously awaited her reply.

Finally, after a silence that had stretched to some length, she said, "Yes, Martha wrote me about it." Then, dropping the subject of the will altogether, she went on, "Gilford and I were there for Luke's funeral, I mean. The weather was bad, but we did make it in time for the service, and everything about it seemed so unreal with the pneumonia taking him so quickly like it did. In fact, Luke was always such a tower of strength and full of life that I don't believe there was one person there that felt that it was him who was being buried, including his wife. Of course, Eliza was so deeply in shock and grief besides that it is a wonder she was able to be there for Luke's burial at all. Martha writes that she is slowly coming back though, and I'm so glad for that. It does take time, you know."

"I can imagine it does, and especially when a couple has been together as long as they had," agreed Whit, disappointed that the subject of the will had affected so few words before it was dropped.

"Well," Lucy said, "We won't see the likes of Luke Heyward again for some time to come, if we even do, because, in my opinion, he was so morally decent, and so kind and wise." She looked toward the stove, adding, "I believe the coffee is ready." She rose from the table and after filling their cups with coffee she sat back down and asked of Whit's activities in recent months.

However, as Whit began talking of his doings between gulps of coffee and hunks of cookies while Lucy kept refilling his coffee cup and sipping on her coffee along with him, he noted long before he said all he had in mind to say, or at least all he desired to say about his doings and particularly to the woman sitting opposite him, that Lucy gave every appearance of letting her mind stray far more to wherever her thoughts had gone to, than listening to what she had asked to be filled in on about his doings! Moreover, she seemed to be deeply pensive about something. So, beginning to feel uncomfortable – a feeling he had never experienced before talking with Miss Lucy – Whit shifted his lean, stalwart frame around a bit and setting his coffee cup down and leaning back in his chair he up and closed the subject about his doings on the spot saying, "I'm afraid that's about the gist of it, Miss Lucy, you know, the far reaches of an ocean doesn't make for that much interest anyway. I feel I've already rattled too long as it is, hardly given you a chance to open your mouth besides boring you half to death, no doubt."

"Oh, no – no!" exclaimed Lucy. "Your talk hasn't bored

me at all. Don't you ever think that! I may appear to be half-listening and I'm sorry for that, but I've taken in every word you've said," she paused, her mind whirling like a wheel, with her telling herself that's only a half-truth Lucy Sloan and you know it! Tell him! A chance like this may never come again! What are you waiting for? Luke opened it, bless his heart in his will, plain as day! Tell him, you won't be betraying anybody! Tell him before it's too late! Heart pounding, she went on, telling herself she must ease her way into telling him, "It's just that, well, I was wondering if this inheritance that Luke left to you in his will is going to affect what plans you may have had for the future?"

"Haven't given it much thought, Miss Lucy," Whit said, taking heart that the subject was back where he wanted it. "I'll wait and see what meets the eye, so to speak, when I get home. It has crossed my mind in recent months to leave the Navy. But now, I don't know."

"You mean the inheritance may change your plans about coming back home? I don't understand." Lucy said.

"Well, not exactly," said Whit, seeing that both of them were playing a cat and mouse game with the other. "It all depends on how Carr and his mother feel about the matter and what we can work out between us. To tell the truth, that's a vast inheritance for someone to just up and leave a person who's not related to them or their family by blood. It's got me a little stumped. Maybe when I get home though, someone will come up with a ready answer. I hope so."

Finding that an easy way to tell him was becoming more difficult by the moment and still holding back, Lucy said, "I suppose it would cause you to raise questions upon questions that you would like some answers to. That's only normal."

"Only normal for an adoptive like me, Miss Lucy, otherwise there would be no cause for questions and wondering why Mr. Luke left me a fortune in his will. Oh, well, maybe if no one else can tell me why he did, Mr. Luke's attorney Bill Cooper can fill me in on all the details."

"No, I don't think so!" Lucy suddenly blurted back, an edge

of defiance lacing every word. "You see, come what may and even at this late date, proprieties must come above all else and rue to the person who doesn't heed that! Love, pain, heartache, truth, justice, and even death included, to society, none of these things measure up like the fixed and formal rule society has set for itself! No, in my opinion your questions will be swept under the rug to lie there and continue to mold as they ever have!" She looked him straight in the eye, her defiance fading and deep regret breaking her voice as she went on and told him, "You – deserve this endowment that Luke Heyward willed to you. You have the right to live at Green Sea as much as Carr, Beth Anne, or anyone else in the Carson family. It's your birthright. Surely, if you've ever given one glance toward Nathan Carson's portrait hanging in the hallway at Green Sea, you must know that, know that's why Matthew Carson adopted you." Tears had begun to gather and trickle down her face, as she continued on, "You – should've – been told long back – I'm so sorry for that – so deeply regret that you weren't – and all that you've had to endure." She gave way to a sob and took her gaze from his and let it fall to her lap.

Reaching across the table and laying his hand upon hers where it gripped the edge of the table in seemingly support, Whit said, "It hasn't been all that bad, Miss Lucy, certainly not as hard for me as it, obviously, has been for you. Please don't be upset on my part. I'll be all right."

Lifting her tear-streaked face and gazing at him again, she said, "Are you sure?"

"I'm sure," he said, "but I'm wondering about you, and I'm also truly sorry that your love for Nathan Carson was so ill-starred. You must have loved him a great, great deal and, come to think of it, that must've been the case regarding your feelings toward me too!" He had saved her the ordeal of coming right out and saying what, apparently, she still was not up to voicing herself and that was she did indeed give birth to him.

Lacking the courage to hold her gaze directly to his once more, she turned her head and, looking across the kitchen at nothing, she said, "Then, after all these long years, you finally know, having been forced as well as bearing the burden of figuring it all out for yourself alone. Will you ever be able to find it in your heart to forgive me? I should've told you myself, told you after you grew up, and especially after Matthew Carson's death. I can see that now, but I'd given my word to Mr. Carson though and well –" her voice faded away and stopped.

The regret, as well as the sadness he saw on her face, affected him deeply. He wanted to comfort her and was hoping what he was suddenly urged to say to her would to some degree, anyway. He said, "You did what you saw was best for all concerned, Miss Lucy, and it worked out so don't fret yourself about it anymore. It wasn't as if you and I were completely separated and never saw one another again. Although I was to have no understanding of the deep bond that I always felt existed between us until I just recently did figure it all out for myself, you and I were exposed to one another rather often during my earlier years, and certainly your decision to allow the Carson's to adopt me saved both of us enduring a lot of scorn that doubtless would have come our way had you chosen otherwise. In my opinion, it takes a strong, caring and loving heart to make a decision such as you made and have borne with it as long as you have."

With his praiseworthy remarks reviving her thwarted courage, Lucy turned her head back to him and said, "You're not just trying to save my feelings and do believe that my allowing the Carson's to adopt you was solely for your own welfare and have your rightful name and enjoy your place in society as you deserve?"

"Of course, I believe that way," assured Whit. "There is one thing that I am wondering about though."

"What's that?" She anxiously asked. "I'll surely tell you if I possibly can."

"Does Mr. Gilford know I'm your son?"

"Gilford's known almost from the first day we became acquainted with one another. Never would I have attempted to have kept it from him. Since the war had turned both our lives totally around from what we had known or had ever hoped for ourselves, we found we had a lot in common and could talk about it with one another in complete ease." She told him.

Sending the woman sitting across the table from him the first smile he had affected for some little while Whit said, "I might've known you would've told him." He rose from his chair, saying, "I'll get on over to the newspaper office and pay my respects to him."

"Yes, he'll be disappointed if he doesn't get the chance to get in a little visiting with you, too, before I call dinner," she said, rising from her chair also and going on to ask, "What's your favorite dish, Whit?"

"Well, I've had to make do with beans so long, Miss Lucy, I've more or less forgotten I've ever had a favorite. In the Navy it's beans and more beans."

They had reached the front door.

She laughed, "I promise then the menu will be void of beans." She suddenly grew serious again, her thoughts, obviously, turning to something that had nothing to do with dinner as she went on, "Just a moment, Whit, I feel compelled to show you something."

She crossed the floor to a small chest sitting beside the wall and pulling open one of its drawers, drew forth, Whit observed, a gold locket attached to a gold chain.

Stepping back to him, she said, snapping the locket open, "Look at this, it's as new-looking as ever in spite of the long years. When Nat and I were unable to find a minister or anyone to marry us that night in Columbia, his first and last leave from the war in Virginia, he up and cut this piece of braid from the sash of his uniform and tied it around my wedding finger only moments before he stepped on the train. I never saw him again."

Observing too that a tiny daguerreotype of Nat Carson's face was also encased in the locket as well, although she never referred to it, Whit said, "I'm so sorry, Miss Lucy."

"Don't be," she promptly came back. "It's been such a long time and as you said, it all worked out and especially for me.

Everything is finally set to rest. You now know and that's the best part along with Gilford's love and respect. Of course, I like to think I still have yours too."

"You bet you do and you always will," smiled Whit, and reaching for her hand, he confirmed his words by pressing it long and hard before he turned and went on across the porch and down the steps.

Feeling as though the morning's brilliant sunlight had risen in her very soul, Lucy Sloan stood and watched Whit's weaving stride for some little while before she turned away, telling herself, I must hurry, because making a more special dinner for the remainder of my life, I'm certain I will not!

And so, most all of two years had come and gone since Lieutenant Commander Whitney Randolph Carson had awakened to the real truth of his begetting and paid a visit to his biological mother in Lexington, Virginia, as well as the rest of his direct bloodline and adoptive relatives and friends in the Carolina Lowcountry. And, what's more, as Lucy Sloan had predicted to her son, once Whit had arrived among his Lowcountry kin, he was to note that not one person among the entire group was anxious to answer one question he had offered on the subject of the late Nathan Carson! In brief, when is came to the status of his relationship with these family members, he saw nothing had changed at all. Yes, despite all that the late Luke Heyward's bequest to him had revealed and posed, everybody had made it plain that they still regarded him as being the adopted son of Matthew and Amy Drakston Carson! Nothing more. Nothing less.

Of course, there had been the ins and outs of the will that had applied to Whit to be discussed and worked out with Eliza Heyward and her son, which Whit had seen to and which to his surprise Eliza nor Carr Heyward had appeared to hold one degree of grievance about, let alone getting on to the business of seeing the matter through and done with. The terms that were worked out and agreed to were that the Heyward's would cash lease Whit's share on a yearly basis until Whit decided he wanted to try his hand at operating his part of the acreage himself and possibly, take up residence at Green Sea to boot. Though Whit had his doubts about living at Green Sea and, in truth, held no readiness to do so because he was positive he would never see the day come when he would prefer Green Sea over Drakston Hall. Although he was fully aware that ever holding any claim to Drakston Hall was out for him because Stuart was its legal heir and following Stuart, Stuart's son, Luke, and this tradition he fully approved of even though he felt Drakston Hall was his home. In fact, not only was Drakston Hall the place where he had grown to manhood and come by so many sweet memories to hold and reflect on in later years, but it was also the place that still housed Amy Drakston Carson, the woman who had raised him and represented what a real mother's love is despite all the credit he had wanted to shower upon Lucy Sloan on the close bond he had ever felt and shared with the latter.

Yes, Amy Drakston Carson was still very much alive and Whit was clear-sighted enough to reason that she was the woman who had nurtured him, drying the tears and stilling the fears of his childhood in that gentle, calm way of hers – a manner like no other to his way of thinking and he had run to her on many an occasion to seek her ministering and words of reassurance that had been so essential to him in those tender years. In addition, although his staying admiration for Lucy Sloan had not eroded one degree, not to mention how much it pleased him to finally know that he was, indeed, the love child of her liaison with the late Nathan Carson instead of some unknown couple whom had ever been nameless to him and would have remained thus, it had taken him no time – once he had pondered all details – to gather the opinion that the hush, hush attitude of both the Carson and Drakston family members regarding the entire delicate matter of his birth was the better and most wise course to have followed after all! For there was no question in Whit's mind that his close bond with Amy Carson had been not only the one substance that had greatly helped heal the scars of her son's death, but he was also positive that the joy she had taken from being in Frank's company was restored somewhat by his own presence when he was granted the opportunity to visit at Drakston Hall.

So, having the foresight to see that airing the facts of the entire matter of his birth and discussing it in this twilight period of Amy Drakston Carson's life – shaking her quiet peace with the impact of an earthquake – would be far more hurtful to her than any advantage he might ever reap since those of whom who were close to him were already on to it and, apparently could not love and respect him more, Whit had pushed the whole disconcerting matter aside and gone on doing the things he usually had done on his visits home.

Holding the distinction of being the most eligible and praiseworthy bachelor that the Lowcountry had seen since the bachelor days of the late Frank Drakston, Whit was feted and dined so often that he began to wonder if his naval uniform would give enough to see him back to his ship. Hardly a day passed that he did not find himself seated opposite some fair maiden – sometimes they were not so fair – at somebody's dinner table. He graciously obliged these same maidens with many a waltz at the numerous balls that were held in his honor. In short, he made sure few wallflowers graced the walls on these occasions, if any! As a guest of both Carr Heyward and Stuart Drakston, he rode to the hounds a number of times. He fished in the river for bream. But most important before the day of his departure dawned, he had journeyed back to Green Sea to go horseback-riding with Eliza Heyward.

Much to Whit's surprise and gratitude, Eliza had suggested the outing and had gone on to tell Whit that they mostly would keep to the riding trails of Green Sea's acreage, because she thought it important that he become more familiar with the lay of Green Sea's lands and especially its northern boundary which connected with Drakston Hall's acreage. However, possessing a deep sense of perception that came near matching Eliza's sixth sense about most things, Whit had sensed right off that something more was on Eliza's mind besides the lay of Green Sea's boundaries. It was instantly clear to Whit that Eliza had had no intention, all along, of letting him depart the

Lowcountry on this visit home without filling him in on every detail that she knew, or surmised, about his birth and adoption as well as the vast inheritance he had come by through Luke Heyward's habit of fair play.

And, talk they had – aunt and nephew of direct bloodline – talking and becoming fully acquainted with one another's fears and misgivings for the future as well as their dreams and hopes, too, like never before.

And now as Eliza Heyward continued to occupy the same rocker that she had settled herself in early that morning, it suddenly startled her to realize that aside from reflecting on that horseback outing with Whit and the letters that had flowed between her and him since that day, there had been little else in her life for almost two years now that would be worth giving a thought to! Yes, her days and her nights, too, had been plenty dull and empty without Luke. But Whit had promised to write often and he had kept his promise, which to her had been a godsend in disguise. To tell the truth, she did not know how she would have made it without Whit's letters, because they were so zestful and soul-lifting they diverted her mind from her grief somewhat. Every sentence that he wrote seemed to stir and actually leap from his letters like a dynamo thundering to life. Granted, she would ever be grateful that she had had the foresight to perceive the day that Whit had called at Green Sea following Luke's death that he had come to feel about as misplaced and befuddled with how things were stacking up as she herself was feeling at the time – something like being in the right church but definitely the wrong pew – and had disclosed all of it to Whit, or as much as she truly knew to be the truth concerning the entire matter of his adoption.

Yes, she had told Whit everything about the whole business of his finally knowing that he was indeed a Carson and was entitled to the inheritance that Luke had left him and had begged his forgiveness that he was forced to figure everything out for himself instead of being told by family members as he should have been long years back. She and Whit had gone to the cemetery and as they had stood beside Nathan Carson's tomb, she had told him everything she could recall about her younger brother. She had done her best to give Whit a mental picture of Nathan Carson the man, his make-up as a whole – the mold of his personality and the way he expressed his thinking and opinions. Whit had appeared to have digested everything she had told him with little difficulty and much understanding and also to have held no bitterness toward any one person. Although there was a striking resemblance of Nathan Carson in Whit's face, she thought to the latter's good fortune his whole make-up appeared to be identical to that of his late grandfather, Matthew Carson, the man who had adopted and raised him. For as Matthew Carson had been able to do and done, Whit also seemed to be able to push the hurdles of life aside and continue on keeping his expectations high as well as eager to meet what came next!

All of a sudden, as Eliza was telling herself that she must move on inside and pen a letter to Whit regarding the latest doings at Green Sea, not to mention that O'Henry's store had been wiped out by fire the day before, she saw a buggy turning off the river road into the drive. Martha had come rushing to Green Sea yesterday to tell them about the loss of the store, with everybody agreeing that without the old familiar landmark gracing the crossroads, the community would never be the same again. She did not know how Martha managed it, but whether the news was good or bad without fail Martha was always at the ready to report it! To tell the truth, in her opinion, Martha was no less informative than an actual newspaper and had always been. And what's more, although she and Martha both had passed their prime long years back, Martha's driving was wild as ever. Despite all the warnings she had mouthed to Martha over the years, the latter had come whirling up the drive yesterday with only one buggy wheel making contact with the drive as she rounded the corner toward the front steps! She had been certain that Martha was not going to escape from being thrown into the porch columns on this occasion and had turned her head to keep from seeing it happen but hearing no screams, she had turned back and as always there was Martha looking as calm as a spring breeze skidding on all four buggy wheels to her usual parking place! She had made up her mind then and there she was through lecturing Martha about her madcap driving ever again. It was time.

Shifting her thoughts from Martha and peering more closely at the approaching buggy, Eliza was almost certain that it was the Jewish peddler Simon Weinstein who called at Green Sea from time to time and throughout the neighborhood, too, plying his dry goods – a custom that had been established during the war and had become more commonplace following the war when so many people lacked the transportation, to say nothing of having the money or the hours to spare to go to town to get the necessary items they were in need of, let alone the luxuries they did purchase before the war. Therefore, any peddler was always made welcome and a place to display their goods – usually on the front porch.

Still, continuing to peer at the approaching buggy, Eliza attached no importance whatever that the horse pulling the buggy was unfamiliar to her, because Simon Weinstein was noted to change horses about as often as the weather changed. And thinking about the numerous times she and Luke had welcomed the peddler and the many dry goods they had always purchased from him, literally bolts of cloth in all kinds of different colors and prints for themselves as well as the tenants and the sharecroppers too, she found her head dropping down and staring at the solid black dress she was wearing and also appearing to be seeing its drab color and make as well for the first time! Although the custom for mourning the dead called for wearing black and black only for at least a year – some never wore anything else but black, like Aunt Amy – Eliza was suddenly brought up short wondering if she had become daft in the head! Why she had swathed herself in black for even a week she was wondering when she knew how much Luke had detested the color? Well, no more, Luke, from this very day will I wear black, if I have to swath myself in a dishcloth, and I surely hope Simon has some pretty cloth, pretty spring colors, even red, to show me! Yes, I hope to be sewing a new dress to wear no later than tomorrow.

And, as her gaze continued to peer at the drabness of her attire and then lifting her head and looking into the distance at nothing, Eliza began to crowd her thoughts with her appearance as a whole, wondering if she presented as unsightly a picture as the cheerless, drab color she was swathed in from head to foot! Yes, doubtless she did, she immediately concluded, and as disconcerting as the thought was, she was certain that it was going to do her more good than harm simply because she was suddenly dressing herself in all kinds of pretty spring bright colors – colors like the pretty rows of phlox blooming in her garden. The purples, the pinks and the whites and blues. Yes, she hoped Simon had a bolt of blue cloth, hopefully a pretty blue silk, among his cloth goods today, so she could start sewing her new dress maybe this very day. That would be a good start until she could go to the dress shops in Charleston! She was going to throw away every piece of black clothing she owned, or give it to the hands if they wanted it. On second thought, if Simon had no kind of blue cloth, she intended to make herself a new dress in some color no later than this afternoon!

Luke had so loved the color blue, always said it brought out the blue in her eyes that much more. And what about that blue negligee? Oh, yes, he had loved her in it too. Had Luke seen through her scheme that night? If he had, he had been too much of a gentleman to ever mention it. Some Christmas Eve that was. She would always hold the memory in her bosom. Though, beginning this very day, she must not hold onto it too tightly. Luke was gone and all they had shared too aside from the memories. She must see and look on all of it like the old Biblical book of Proverbs states, "A time to weep and a time to mourn." And she must heed the saying and try not to weep and mourn so much. Was it not like Martha's driving anyway? No matter how much she wept, it was not going to change one thing regarding Luke's absence from her life.

Come to think on it, although there had been far more good than bad as Luke had pointed out in his letter, her and Luke's marriage had not been joy and bliss every day to the week anyhow. She had no idea why her mind always skipped the bad and had simply refused to acknowledge there had been discord between them at times. It could be that she had, unconsciously, done that in order to survive the grief, outlast it and still be in one piece, whole, so to speak, instead of coming apart altogether – aware of not much of anything anymore! Yes, she thought perhaps that was it, why one only thought of the pleasant in their grief instead of the unpleasant things like she had done.

In any case, she must admit there had been distance and misery, too, between her and Luke at times, hardship as well upon them and mostly because of Frank's jealousness of Luke and the former's evil doings, which sadly had resulted into tragic circumstances and ended Frank's life at the young age of twenty-nine years old. However, despite everything that had fallen regarding Frank and his doings, she had come to believe that Frank did feel a deep abiding love for her that had nothing to do with physical desire because of his concern over her giving birth to Jane Anne at Drakston Hall and remaining in Drakston Hall's comfort for a while anyway rather than her being at Green Sea in her confinement. Frank saw the house that Luke had built for them to live in after the mansion had burned as nothing but a shanty and too uncomfortable for her in any case let alone for her confinement. At any rate, she was certain no woman could have looked less seductive than she had on that day and Frank had been truly concerned for her welfare, and more important, it was not Frank's nature to plead or humble himself to anybody as he had done that day. But when she had turned a deaf ear to his rare act of generosity, he had abruptly left and gone on to Charleston and pulled a drunk for three long days!

Still, as much as she was regretful for so many things that were too late to change, she was also deeply thankful for that short while that day at Drakston Hall when she and Frank were given the chance to talk alone together although the circumstances could not have been more painful for both of

Louise Gore Sayre-David

them – his physical pain that was to take his life only a day away, and her emotional pain that was too long a time in coming to any degree of healing. For the short while they were granted that day, it seemed they were sharing a mellow harmony that always been there between them, but instead of responding to it emotionally and giving it a chance to develop into a close relationship, some hidden substance in both of them had caused them to clash constantly at one another. Yes, for the short while it was, she felt that she and Frank both had reached out emotionally, and had embraced one another with deep feeling for the first time in their lives on that dreadful day. Though there had not been any physical contact whatever between them, the feeling had persisted and she would ever be thankful.

All at once, Eliza was letting her memories of Frank go when she realized the approaching buggy had stopped at the hitching post instead of proceeding on around the drive and stopping at the front steps as Simon Weinstein had always done. The front veranda had ever served the peddler as a handy place to display his wares, not to mention that it saved him a lot of steps when unloading his goods and placing them back in his buggy again. So, with her expectations of sewing herself a new dress and shedding the black garb she was wearing falling to nothing, she peered more closely at the tall, lanky well-dressed gentleman leaping from the buggy and already looping his horse's reins over the hitching post rail. Doubtless a lawyer who had stopped to see Carr about something she was telling herself when upon his first step toward her she suddenly felt her heart give a lurch and felt that it had lodged in her throat – Bill Clarendon! Yes, the question of his identity was plain in that unmistakable limp that had stayed with him since the Battle of Shiloh! She had not the faintest idea when she had last seen him, or for that matter even thought of him.

But, even so, as Eliza rose from her rocker and stepped to the edge of the porch waiting for Bill Clarendon to close the distance between them, she began to fight hard against a sudden urge of wanting to cry, which truly baffled her even more than she regretted Bill seeing her looking so drab and unkempt in her awful black dress. But if Bill Clarendon noticed anything about her appearance or what she was wearing – the color or anything else about it – his joy and happiness at seeing her again and being able to offer his hand to her blotted it out on the spot as he said, reaching the front steps and stretching out his hand to her as Eliza was stepping off the porch and onto the first doorstep to offer her hand to him, "I took a chance on seeing you, Eliza, but never did I dream I'd be so lucky as to find you on the front porch like this. It's so wonderful to see you again, dear, and looking as well as you do."

The radiance in his gaze did not escape Eliza. Trying hard to hold back the tears she felt gathering in her eyes and forcing herself to smile, Eliza said, her obvious emotion moving Bill Clarendon deeply, "And I never would have dreamed you were driving that buggy. I thought you were Simon Weinstein making his rounds, and I was thinking about buying some new dress goods and sewing a new dress and get out of this drab dishrag that I'm wearing!"

Instantly, letting that throaty laugh of his fill the air – the sound of it taking Eliza back long years past – Bill, on the verge of asking her if she was disappointed that he was not the peddler but thinking better of it, said instead, "Well, dishrag or no dishrag, it feels good to be looking at you, Eliza, and seeing, too, that the years have changed you so little. Not like some in our age group including me."

All at once, Eliza felt as though she had truly stepped back in time, experiencing that same calm and sense of well-being that had ever served to envelope her when in Bill Clarendon's presence.

"No, not you, Bill," she said, as she, involuntarily, brushed back a curl that had strayed from her still lush hair piled atop her head. "I'd know you any time, place or anywhere."

"You're too kind." he smiled, "The same gracious Eliza, as reluctant as ever not to hurt my feelings, but thanks anyway."

Though she had told him the truth, she was also observing his once deep, blond hair was totally white but hindered his appearance none whatsoever as she returned his smile, which was no longer hard for her to effect, and told him, "No, nothing of the kind. The years have been good to you." She took her hand from his. "But I am going to suggest we move on to the porch where we can continue our talk sitting in comfort instead of standing here on the steps wearing our legs and feet out!"

Totally at ease with one another and sharing a laugh they moved on to the porch and took their seats, with Bill stretching out his wounded leg in a more comfortable position as he replied to Eliza's inquiring of his sister Charlotte, "I'm grateful I can say, Eliza, that Charlotte's well and appears to be much contented with her station in life. It took a good many years for her to accept the fact that the war did come and before it ended had, indeed, turned all our lives on a different course."

"Indeed, it did," agreed Eliza, "and cut so many lives short in the process."

"Yes, unfortunately, and Orr Camden's untimely death hit Charlotte a hard blow. But thank God she finally reached the point one day where she could be counted among the war's many survivors, which of course, reminds me of Lucy Randolph Sloan. I trust both she and her husband are enjoying good health and having a successful newspaper business in Lexington." Bill said.

"Yes, they're both well, and their publishing business is running smoothly, too, I understand," replied Eliza, going further to add, "I mostly hear of them through Phil though. Phil and Gilford met one another a few years after the war and have maintained a close relationship ever since. In fact, they're like family, close as two brothers despite the fact they were complete strangers to one another when they met. Speaking of the war, Gilford Sloan lost his entire family because of it. I guess one could say in the war's aftermath, he and Phil both were lost and searching and having those two things in common bonded them together and sealed their friendship. And, I see it like a miracle from heaven, too, that Gilford Sloan and Lucy found one another. Lucy helps Gilford with their business and is also involved in church and social work. For several years now she's had a full and happy life after so many years of grief and loneliness and I'm so thankful for her blessings."

"As likewise to Charlotte, too, I'm thinking," said Bill. "She's also much involved with church and community work, too, plus the duties of running a household. Would you believe that she mostly saw to all the outside needs of the entire plantation while I was in Europe well over a year? She did a mighty fine job of it, too, if I do say so with pride."

"You've been to Europe and were away well over a year?" asked Eliza, her voice laced with surprise and wonder, too, mentally asking herself why had not Mollie Cooper said one word about her brother being in Europe, not to mention for that long a time to boot! Then, it came to her like a shot! Mollie probably had mentioned it and other things, too, but she doubted she had not heard much of anything that Mollie and others as well had said for way too long while visiting her. It was like this drab dress she was swathed in! Well, it was time she woke up from wherever she had been and start paying more attention to the present, like Bill telling her now.

"Yes, I was over there a lot longer than I had planned on," said Bill. "I had a lot of business to see to, and I did a lot of sightseeing as well on this trip over there, doing the sightseeing in Austria and Switzerland mostly. That's why I stayed as long as I did. Eliza, the Swiss Alps were some sight to see and take in. I wish you could see them, some experience to behold."

I can imagine they are." Eliza said. Then out of the blue, she blurted, "I've always wanted to go to Europe!" startling herself for mouthing such a declaration because, to her recollection, she had never given one thought to going to Europe before.

Surprised too, Bill came back saying, "I had no idea you felt that way, Eliza, I guess I've always thought of you as having no interest in being any place but here at Green Sea." He was silently telling himself that despite his knowing Eliza as long as he could remember, he was finding out that he truly knew her not at all!

She threw him again.

"Well," she laughed, "I must be honest and tell you that I haven't felt that I've wanted to go until just now when you mentioned the Swiss Alps."

"Oh, I see," laughed Bill as well, taking on that same easy comfort that had ever been there between him and Eliza – a reclaiming of those bonds of harmony that had ever been there for both of them when in one another's company. However, no sooner than Bill and Eliza both had recognized they were as like-minded as always, the discovery fusing their feelings to an unhoped for high, Matt's sudden breakneck reappearance on his pony grabbed both their attention so that it was as though those sensations of delight were nothing but pure imagination and had never been.

Instantly, on her feet, Eliza was shouting, "Look out, Matt, you're going to run smack into that tree if you aren't more careful!" When she saw that Matt had stopped the pony only seconds before slamming into one of the large oaks on the drive and was already dismounting from the pony's back, she spilled a long sigh and added, "I declare that child's driving is as wild as Martha's. Too often, he scares me half to death." She fell back down in her chair and Bill, who had also been brought to his feet by Matt's recklessness, followed suit.

Bounding up the steps and on across the porch, Matt, breaking his pace to a stop in front of Bill's chair, said, "Mister, does that horse there at the hitching post belong to you? I like horses a lot better than I like ponies. Ponies are for babies, but I have to ride one because my Pa won't let me have a horse yet."

Offering Matt his hand, Bill laughed, "Yes, that horse happens to be mine, and I take it that you like the looks of him. I'm Bill Clarendon, young fellow. I'm glad to make your acquaintance."

"Matt, Mr. Clarendon is an old friend of mine." Eliza enjoined, hoping as she mouthed the information that Green Sea's rough-and-tumble heir would mind his manners and do the family proud.

"Yes, Ma'am," Matt said, stretching his fingers out as far as they would give so his hand would look more grown-up in comparison with Bill Clarendon's as he gave it to Bill and went on to say "I'm Matt Heyward. My name's Matthew but everybody shortened Matthew to Matt and you may, too, sir, if you like."

Eliza, looking on, gave a sigh under her breath and simply beamed in prideful delight.

Giving Matt a generous handshake, Bill said, "Well thank you, Matt. I feel honored and will very much like addressing you as Matt. I assume you were named after your great-grandfather Matthew."

"Yes, sir, that's what they tell me," affirmed Matt, as he drew his hand away from Bill's and slid it into the pocket of his overalls. Then after giving Bill Clarendon a close rake over from head to foot with his intense deep-blue gaze, he promptly inquired, "Are you a courting friend of Grandmother's? I hope you are because Grandmother has cried bushels since Grandpop went to heaven." His handsome expression was set in dead earnest.

"M—att! For heaven's sa—kes!" Eliza sputtered, as completely undone as Bill Clarendon appeared to be. "It truly beats me how you come up with such outlandish remarks as you do."

"But I didn't come up with it, Grandmother, Aunt Martha did. I heard Aunt Martha say that what you needed was a courting friend and for you not to be surprised if she sent you one!" Matt solemnly declared.

"Mar—tha—wh—en—wh—ere?" Eliza continued to sputter, her face looking as though she had emptied a full box of rouge on it. "Never mind! At times your Aunt Martha talks when she should be listening and that goes for you, too, young man!"

"Yes, Grandmother," muttered Matt, unable to understand why his simple question had gotten his grandmother's ire up so? He wanted to get to himself so he could give more thought to his mistake in asking the question in the first place. "Can I go now?" he chanced to add.

"May, Matthew, not can." Eliza promptly corrected, her patience with Matt pulsing to a mere trickle. "And, no you may not! Besides, it's too near dinner time for you to go sauntering off some place. Take that chair there and try to keep out of mischief till dinner is called."

"Yes, Grandmother," muttered Matt once again as he turned and finding the nearest empty chair, took his seat and crossed his hands in his lap. His head was more than full with puzzling questions. Never could he remember hearing his grandmother address him as Matthew before. He wondered why that was, almost forgetting Bill Clarendon who in his opinion had caused the whole uproar in the first place. He began to wish that Grandmother's old friend had kept his fine horse headed in some other direction!

Swiftly transferring her attention from her thwarted grandson to a somewhat disconcerted Bill Clarendon, Eliza, trying to steady the jolt of Matt's question, said, "Bill, will you stay and have dinner with us? I think I heard Pete say something about fried chicken." Then, to Matt's astonishment, she looked at him again and putting on a quick smile, added, "I think Matt's taken a liking to you and would very much like having the opportunity to become better acquainted with you."

"Of course," Bill smiled back. "The pleasure will be mine, not only to partake of Pete's fried chicken, but to engage more in talking with this young man here."

"Well good," Eliza said, "I'll go to tell Pete to set an extra plate." And unable to hold her displeasure with her adored grandson any longer and wanting to compensate for it in some way, she silently let her expression explain her feelings to Bill as she added, "Perhaps while I'm gone, you'd like to give Matt a closer look at that splendid horse you're driving."

"Certainly, I'll be happy to" Bill came back and springing to his feet, he offered Matt his hand and went on, "Come on Matt, we'll go and give him a good look over."

Quickly springing to his feet too Matt could hardly believe his good fortune. Besides having fallen back into the good graces of his grandmother without saying one word or doing any kind of penance whatever, like bringing in wood for the stove, he was going to get the chance to ask this gentleman all the questions he wanted about that fine horse at the hitching post, but also that courting business about his grandmother too!

Suddenly, full of glee, Matt was no longer wishing that Bill Clarendon had not stopped at Green Sea.

Starting through the doorway, Eliza turned back and, looking at the older man and young child with their hands locked together walking across the yard toward the hitching post, had she not known better, the tall slender man with his shock of white hair could very well have been Luke, because she had seen the latter walking with Matt in the same way so many times. Feeling the grief starting to well in her heart as full as ever, she pressed hard against it and turning away went on down the hall toward the kitchen. She was resolved to hold fast to find a more cheerful existence for herself – walk away from the shadows and enjoy the sunlight more. Still, the strength of her will to do just that was put to the test sooner than she had counted on.

The noonday meal turned out to be a most pleasant affair. Eliza was seated in her usual place at the end of the table. The chair at the other end of the table was occupied by Carr Heyward. At his mother's suggestion, Carr had moved into the chair upon his father's death. Bill Clarendon was seated an easy distance to the left of Eliza's chair, with Beth Anne Heyward seated to the right of her husband, while Matt was to his father's left facing his mother across the table. The chair that Phil Carson normally occupied, which was to Eliza's right and parallel with Matt's, was empty.

Phil Carson's absence from the dinner table was not unusual and certainly nothing to cause the other family members to be concerned about. In short, they were becoming accustomed to his empty chair and rather often at that. For this was just another day that Phil had announced he was heading to Drakston Hall and he would not be returning until late afternoon. Yes, he would dine at Drakston Hall at dinner time.

Yes, he would be back at Green Sea for supper, and, more often than not, and despite the fact nobody had yet to raise the question, Phil would go on and volunteer the news that he must check on Amy Drakston Carson, his elderly aunt and late father's widow, despite the fact that Amy Carson was continuing her normal lifestyle and interest and surrounded by a number of other family members as well. Though it was obvious she continued to mourn Matthew Carson's absence. At any rate, Phil might as well have added nothing more concerning his going to Drakston Hall so often. For his announcement to check on Amy Carson never failed to bring a knowing smile between Eliza and Beth Anne Heyward. They both were on to the growing close relationship between Phil and Elizabeth Drakston, Frank Drakston's widow, which, of course, both Eliza and Phil Carson's daughter approved of and were happy about. Although Eliza could not help seeing the match of Phil and Elizabeth somewhat ironic, taking into account that the late Frank Drakston had so little admiration for all the Carson men. Granted, the thought of Elizabeth Drakston becoming a Carson and taking up residence at Green Sea and living no longer at Drakston Hall was a little hard for Eliza to digest just yet.

At all events, the dinner hour had progressed along on a most pleasant scale. Matt had devoured his fried chicken leg and rice and black-eyed peas, as well as Pete's fresh blueberry pie, without mishap. Though by the time he was emptying his plate he had begun to nod. And at Beth Anne's suggestion Bessie was shepherding him off to the nursery for his nap. Matt, at six years of age, did not succumb to a nap every day. But his peppiness on this day had finally conquered his energy and the task of fighting to keep his eyelids open any longer had been too much for him. Yes, Bessie was still an abiding presence at Green Sea and so was Sam her husband.

Anyway, dinner was finally over with and everybody had moved from the dining room to the front parlor with Carr and Beth Anne in a short while announcing they must get back to working on some legal documents and making their excuses and leaving Eliza and Bill Clarendon alone together once more.

Already on his feet since good form called for it when Carr and Beth Anne had left the parlor, Bill was delighting in the thought of visiting with Eliza for at least an hour longer when it came to him like the rush of a freight train, that he had told his sister, Charlotte, that he would be back home long hours before. Thus, he said, "I must be on my way, too, Eliza. It's just come to me that I told Charlotte I'd be back hours ago. I'd completely forgotten it. I'd better be on my way before she has someone out looking for me. I've enjoyed your company again so much, to say nothing of Matt's, Carr and his wife too, that my mind's slipped up on me." He offered Eliza his hand.

Meeting his hand briefly, Eliza said, "Your company's been our pleasure too, Bill. And thanks for taking so much time with Matt and entertaining him as you have. I'm afraid the subject of horses is going to take priority with him for some time to come. I hope he didn't wear on you too much."

"Certainly not," Bill assured. "His liveliness is good for me, airs out the stale corners in my mind, I'd say. I enjoyed being with him." Bill paused, appearing to have something else on his mind. Then he added, "Eliza, he reminds me of Mr. Matthew, not only in his looks but in his ways too."

"So, you can see it too," Eliza said. "I've wondered at times if I were seeing the close resemblance of my father because I wanted it to be true."

"No, my dear," smiled Bill. "I can assure you, you aren't overusing your imagination because the likeness is there and very distinct at that. Well, thanks again for a wonderful visit, I must be on my way."

However, instead of moving on toward the door, Bill Clarendon hesitated, giving every indication he wanted to say something else but was trying to find the courage to give voice to it. Then just as it seemed an awkward silence was beginning to fall, he said, phrasing his say hardly any different than a bashful schoolboy, "Uh, Eliza, I just thought of something, I wonder – well, we're having a social at my church this coming Saturday, and all-day affair – you know – there's going to be a cake walk, a sack race, even a horseshoe contest for the men and lots of other entertainment and games. Well, I just thought that maybe you'd consider going. I'd feel honored to have you there as my guest." His gaze had beome more hopeful with every labored word.

"I – think – not, Bill – I -- ," her wavering response had stopped altogether, telling Bill Clarendon nothing definite.

Undaunted, Bill promptly disclosed, "Oh, I forgot to explain that it's to benefit a family in our community who got burned out a few days ago, lost everything they owned but their mule and cow. The man risked his life and got his hands burned saving those."

"Oh! That's terrible," cried Eliza. "Could I help, donate some clothing, bedding and a little money perhaps? I'll gather everything up and send it by Sam. Where shall he take it to, the church?"

Bill got the message. She had turned him down flat as dirt.

Feeling as though he were some old tattered coat that Eliza Heyward had just thrown in a heap of rags, Bill said, "Well, I'm sure they will appreciate anything you might give, but I didn't mean to sound as if I'm out canvassing the whole countryside on their behalf. I just thought you might enjoy the fellowship, that's all. If you do wish to contribute though, you could have Sam bring everything to the church Saturday. There'll be a committee there to take care of it. I really must be on my way." He turned and began to walk toward the doorway.

Eliza walked with him, sensing his hurt and disappointment as they went on through the hall and front doorway and on across the porch in silence. It bothered her. Not only did she feel that she had soured every aspect of his visit for him, but she also reasoned that in all probability there would never be another invitation of any kind from Bill Clarendon to reject!

They had reached the front steps. Turning to Eliza and offering her his hand once more, Bill said "Sorry you can't join us Saturday, Eliza. I believe you would have enjoyed it. You take care of yourself." And as this farewell was slicing the air between them – distancing the harmony they had always shared by more than the miles that would separate them from the other, Eliza suddenly sensed, Bill pulled his hand from hers and began covering the steps taking two at a time.

Hardly realizing what she was doing or would have recognized the voice as being that of her own, Eliza was suddenly dashing down the steps after Bill Clarendon and hollering for him to wait. Further, she had no idea what she was going to tell him for the moment or anything else that might come to her. The one thing that she did know and was certain of was that she could not let him leave without setting things right – try to restore their relationship to the easy level they had ever shared and what she had destroyed, for whatever degree it was!

However, as Bill turned back to her voice, Eliza was almost as startled as he was when she heard herself blurting to him in an almost breathless voice, "Bill, on second thought, I believe I'll enjoy the fellowship too! I'll be looking forward to being there."

"Splendid," he smiled. "I'll be looking forward to escorting you." Still, Eliza was not so sure when she saw him drop his smile all of a sudden and appeared to be thinking about something else that had nothing to do with them being together when he went on to say, "Eliza, I've just thought of something."

"What's that?" she asked, somewhat anxiously.

"Let's take Matt with us."

"Oh, he'd love it, Bill" How kind he was she thought. "Thank you for suggesting it. I'll tell Matt first thing when he wakes up from his nap."

"Well, like I said, Matt's as refreshing as a cool glass of lemonade. No, seriously, I promised him I'd let him drive my horse at the first opportunity that fell our way. Now I'll have the chance to keep my word to him. You and I are both old enough to know that keeping a promise to a child is most important," he smiled.

"Yes." Eliza smiled back. "And Matt and I will be waiting early Saturday."

"I'll be here," he said.

Going back up the steps, Eliza was sorta taken aback when she heard Bill Clarendon suddenly begin to whistle the poignant, closing notes of the marching song "Dixie."

Time and its change, thought Eliza, as she kept on ascending the steps.

Chapter Three

The weather had turned freezing cold overnight. But, even so, Eliza thought she had never seen the sky look more brilliant, or the frost-capped landscape glistening like a diamond in early sunrise more inviting than it did on this cold January morning. Having no idea when she would have the opportunity to do so again, if indeed she ever would from the same spot, Eliza had stood at her bedroom window for some little while now shivering and hugging herself tighter and tighter as she gazed upon the familiar scene and tried to fasten it in her memory as tight and secure as a nail hammered into a board.

No, Eliza Heyward's shivers had nothing at all to do with the cold weather considering that the fireplace grate had been seen to and stirred back to life some hours earlier and the room was plenty warm enough. She was shivering from a bad case of nerves brought on by a combination of a number of things all mingled together. There was fear of the unknown along with despair too, as well as concern and yes, hope and expectation also. And, on top of all these things, she could not help feeling she had turned into a coward with no courage whatever and had taken on the falseness of being a hypocrite besides! Moreover, to make matters worse, she was well aware she should be basking in a transport of delight only and wanted to be as much as she had ever wanted anything in her entire life but finding one degree of that elated feeling she yearned for appeared to be as remote as trying to make her way to the moon. For this was the day she was to become the wife of William "Bill" Clarendon her ever friend and childhood sweetheart! In addition, one might add that the prospective groom was doubtless the most eligible and highly respectable man in the whole county, if not the entire state of South Carolina, and most women in spite of an age factor or anything else not only would be overjoyed to have his love but jump at the chance to marry him to boot!

Yes, as incredible as it was on this cold January Sunday morning, immediately following the worship service at the Baptist church as her late father and Aunt Amy Drakston had done long years ago, she and Bill Clarendon were slated to walk down the church aisle to the altar together to repeat their marriage vows with the Reverend Marsh Reed presiding and in the presence of the congregation. Moreover, following the ceremony, and in the same tradition again that her father and aunt had adhered to, she and Bill and their wedding guests were to journey back to Green Sea for a midday wedding celebration feast and the cutting of the bridal cake as well, all of which was going to be supervised by no other than Cousin Martha Drakston Randolph, of course!

Yes indeed, Martha Randolph was still very much on the scene and, with the exuberance of a child at its first birthday party, had taken charge of the entire affair. However, despite the integral role Martha had and did play in Eliza's life and especially at this late date in their relationship when Eliza had long become cushioned to Martha's candor and near childlike behavior at times and thought nothing of it, the former was truly left aghast the day she told Martha about Bill Clarendon's proposal and without batting an eye Martha shrieked, "Oh, Eliza, that's the best news I've heard since the war ended! How excited you must feel! How I wish I could get married again!"

With Martha's last thoughtless statement shaking her from head to feet as well as rousing a degree of resentment in her too, Eliza screeched back, hardly realizing what she was saying, "Martha! You are married! Do you realize what you've just said? Come to your senses!"

Looking as innocent and put down as a hurt child, Martha said, "Well, I should think since I am aware of where I am and what I'm doing and saying that I do have my senses every last one of them, if I do say so, thank heavens!"

"But Bruce is still very much alive, and you and he are still husband and wife together, so I find your remark about marrying again hard to understand, to say the least." Eliza protested.

"Bruce has nothing to do with my remark," flared Martha. "I love Bruce Randolph's very toenails, even the part he trims off and throws away, Eliza, and you know it!"

"Well, yes, that's certainly been my feelings from the day you married Bruce," allowed Eliza. "That's why I'm shocked at your remark."

"All right, then, forget the marrying part and just say have an affair!" Martha dared to blurt. Then with a mischievous grin replacing all other feelings on her face, she went on, "Haven't you ever thought about having an affair on the side, Eliza? Now, nothing permanent, mind you! Just some man other than one's husband for a change of pace once in a while that's all! Oh, I forget, where there's attraction between the two parties, naturally. Think about the thrills that kind of slipping around would serve one!"

More aghast than ever at Martha's daring talk, Eliza muttered, "No, I've never entertained one thought about having an affair going on the side, Martha, and frankly I don't think you have either. Furthermore, I think things of that nature are too private and serious to joke about! And besides, with Luke, I've already known all the thrills I should ever want to know or ever yearn to experience, I should think."

Dropping her amused expression on the instant, Martha said, "Well, not only will I take your word for that, but I might've known that it's impossible to discuss anything with you without your bringing Luke, God rest his soul, into the conversation. You didn't understand one thing I was saying or trying to get across to you, anyhow. So, let's get off the subject and talk about what started it in the first place. Now, tell me, what did you say to Bill Clarendon's proposal? You did say yes, did you not?"

"Not yet, I told him I'd have to have more time to think." Eliza said.

"More time to think," repeated Martha. "Good Lord, Eliza, is that the best you could do? It's a wonder to me that Bill Clarendon didn't tell you that he wasn't interested in time, that he wanted a yes or a no, on the spot. The fact is, you'd better start considering one of the most important factors involved and that is the matter of age! Yes, Eliza, I said age! Both you and Bill are beginning to count your fifties, and God forbid, that is not young any more. I should think that factor alone would cause your brain to work a little faster! Something else, Eliza, a chance to marry again at our age, and especially when the prospective groom happens to be someone of Bill Clarendon's standing, falls few times and far between in one's lifetime, if it ever falls at all! That's another particular that should persuade you to say yes to Bill's proposal before he decides to give up and fly the coop for all time!"

Obviously, beginning to weigh Martha's remarks in earnest, Eliza said, "I know, Martha, and of course, you're right. I promise, I'll give Bill my answer right away."

"Well, for heaven sakes, don't say no!" stormed Martha, her frustration at Eliza's lack of excitement having nearly driven her voice to a screaming pitch. "You and Bill need one another. However, taking into account how often the two of you have been together these past months, I should think that both of you are normal enough to have already seen that without my pointing it out. Heavens! I know I would!"

And, the subject of Bill Clarendon's proposal had continued on between the two cousins for some little while, with Martha daring to go even further than she had already in expressing her liberal-minded views as Eliza mostly listened and still refrained from disclosing the doubts and fears that were causing her hesitation about marrying again.

For one thing, it had not been necessary for Martha to point out to Eliza the aspect of Bill Clarendon's worthiness. She was more than aware of his good qualities and knew he deserved the very best that any wife was capable of giving in a marriage and she was not so sure even at this late date that she could fulfill the role. Granted, becoming mistress of Clarendon Plantation and carrying out the duties that this position would demand of her had not one thing to do with her reluctance to say yes to Bill Clarendon's desire to have her as his wife. For she had been used to the workings of a household for long years, actually upon the sudden death of her mother at the young age of seventeen years old! The one thing that was putting a damper on her misgivings concerning the marriage factor was the question of her physical attraction for Bill and his for her. For, although she and Bill had been courting for months, as her grandson Matt insisted on saying, never once had Bill let his feelings for her go beyond a quick hug or a peck on the cheek! In short, she had begun to wonder if Bill's thoughts on marriage were based more on ideals and spiritualism than realism. To sum it up, her view in regard to the institution of marriage went far beyond a couple being comfortable with one another and making the social rounds and entertaining guests. The physical factor in a marriage was most important too, and so far, Bill's behavior relative to his feelings about that had told her nothing. Though Bill had been overly courteous, actually behaving as if she were some sort of delicate china that he must handle with care lest she break to pieces before his eyes, no demonstration of passion had he shown so far. Of course, she did reason that her grandson's presence could account for Bill's behavior, because Matt was with them most every minute that she and Bill were together. Bill truly adored Matt and Matt returned his devotion. The fact was, this very thing in itself – the closeness between Bill and Matt – had begun to nip at her conscious too. For it was obvious that Bill Clarendon adored children and was so natural and at ease with them that she had begun to wonder that it might be best that he find a wife who was young enough to give him a child of his own. For it was a sure thing a marriage between Bill and herself was not going to produce any Clarendon offspring! Then on top of the age factor and the amorous element in the relationship as well as there would be no child for Bill Clarendon in regard to herself, there was the question of how was she going to feel about leaving Green Sea? Never had she lived any place else. Could she live at Clarendon Plantation and be content? Would she be able to adjust?

At all events, following that talk between her and Martha a

109

short while back, on the very next visit that Bill had made to Green Sea, she had told him that she would marry him! Just like that! As if all those doubts, fears and questions had never been.

Now, fully aware that all those questions and misgivings had gone no place and were still waiting to be answered, Eliza was assailed with more questions and deep concern about leaving Green Sea and living at Clarendon Plantation. And yet, being sensible enough to realize that only the future held the answer to everything, she turned from the window to only be reminded that the hour leaving Green Sea was upon her, considering all the trunks, shoe and hat boxes, she was forced to make her way around packed -- with her clothes and personal things – in order to get to her rocking chair by the hearth to try to pull herself together before leaving for the Baptist church! Still, instantly being flooded with memories of her taking to her rocking chair on her wedding night to Luke, she jumped up from its comfort and darted across the room to where a large mahogany bureau rested against the wall, gripping onto the edge of its top drawer with both hands in an effort to calm and steady her shudders as she tried to focus her thoughts on something else besides herself! For example, her brother, Phil Carson.

Phil Carson was to accompany Eliza to church. She thought maybe Phil had suggested that he and she ride alone together in his coach, instead of her riding with the other family members in the Heyward coach, so as to give her a better chance to relax and also talk about any anxieties that might be plaguing her. For she was certain that Phil was already wise to the turmoil she was enduring. Their status in life had become too parallel for him not to identify with all the things that were weighing on her on this day. Though Phil continued to claim his going to Drakston Hall so much was to visit with their Aunt Amy, everybody who knew Phil was on to the real reason why he was going to Drakston Hall so often, which, of course, was his attraction and interest in Elizabeth Drakston, the late Frank Drakston's widow! Although everybody went along with Phil and pretended otherwise, herself included, nobody was left in doubt that Phil had fallen in love again and as ironic as it was, with Elizabeth Drakston to boot! And, giving thought to Phil and Elizabeth finding happiness and contentment together and not continuing to endure being alone, and feeling grateful that they had come to find love again, Eliza suddenly became aware that her shudders had nearly disappeared as she raised her head and began to study the reflection revealed to her in the mirror before her.

Never having been a vain person in the least regarding her extraordinarily inviting features – an unusually appealing facial beauty – Eliza began to study the image looking back at her and was instantly pleased and thankful at what the mirror was reflecting to her and especially on this particular day. It pleased her to see that the mauve pink woolen suit, which she had chosen to be married in and which she had already donned could not have enhanced her overall features any better, and even though she had no idea what color Bill Clarendon favored, she found herself hoping that he did favor pink. One thing that was and had been a certainty with her when she chose her wedding outfit that it would not be blue – Luke's favorite color. Well, she thought, as she continued to look at her reflection, at the very least, she was not wearing black anymore and was almost certain she never would again, no matter the circumstances – the thought nearly bringing on her shudders again, but still striving not to let the past triumph over the present on this day, she reached for the elegant mauve pink hat which matched her pink suit and which was lying atop the bureau, and placed it on her head, and suddenly, a peal of laughter that could not have come from anyone but her Cousin Martha out in the hallway promptly wiped everything else from Eliza's mind save her immediate wish that before the day came to its close that some of Martha's mirth might penetrate the wall and fasten on her.

Yes, to be sure, Martha Randolph had come to Green Sea at the crack of dawn, and considering all the giggling that Martha had done since her arrival – prompting Bessie and several other women on the plantation who were helping with all the fixings that day to follow suit – Eliza was hard put to see how Martha had been able to announce some time before that all was ready and waiting for the midday wedding feast. Moreover, Eliza had thought she was never going to get all her clothes on because of Martha's interruptions, her flouncing in and out of the bedroom every minute or two as she declared that no tradition for a bride was going to be overlooked! In fact, by this hour, Eliza was certain that Martha had begun to suffer from a degree of lightheadedness, because she was sure that Martha had had a nip of spirits to have kept going at the pace she had. For Eliza, and probably a number of others, was well aware that Martha was not above stealing a little energy, Martha's saying not hers, from the bourbon bottle every now and then.

To please Martha, relative to the tradition of a bride wearing something old, something new, something used and something blue, Eliza had agreed to use Martha's blue topaz hatpin to hold her hat on her head and carry the lace handkerchief that Maggie had carried at her wedding to Seth Junior. No, in point of something used, Eliza had affirmed she was wearing her own garters and, of course, her wedding outfit would do for something new. So, finally, Martha had agreed and said she supposed the problem of the tradition business had been solved and had left Eliza to finish dressing for her wedding.

It went without saying, Eliza Heyward was well aware that her Cousin Martha's views and opinions had always had a great impact on most every move and important decision – not to mention the lesser doubts and questions too – that she had ever agonized over during her lifetime so far. For instance, Eliza was certain now that had it not been for Martha's prompting on the day she had told Martha about Bill's proposal that she would have taken more time in thinking the matter over. Now too late, she recognized she had taken on too many fears, doubts and questions about embarking on a completely new existence from the way she had come to live with herself since

Luke's death. All the same, she took another long look at herself in the mirror and picked up her hat and placed it on her head, making sure that it was firmly secured with Martha's hatpin. Then, determined to carry through with her marriage to Bill Clarendon and all, if anything, that awaited her, she squared her shoulders and was taking her first step to leave the room when she heard Phil Carson call, "Sis, it's about time for us to start out. Are you ready?"

"Coming, Phil," Eliza called back, and stepped on to the door and turned the doorknob without looking back once.

Shifting his gaze from his pocket watch and letting it rest on Eliza as she appeared before him, Phil said, as he took on an expression of astonishment, "Eliza, I swear, if I didn't know differently, I'd say you had not counted your fortieth birthday yet. You look absolutely marvelous. At least fifteen years short from your last birthday. Of course, you've always been pretty, but seeing how lovely you look today makes me wonder if Bill Clarendon is aware of how really attractive you are. He's one lucky man."

Before Eliza could even get her mouth open to reply to Phil's remarks, Martha, rushing out into the hallway from a large linen closet, enjoined, "Well, if he doesn't know how comely Eliza is by this late date, he'd do himself a favor to see his eye doctor! And, certainly, he's lucky to be finally marrying at his age, and that goes for Eliza too! If you ask me, not one in a thousand walk down a church aisle to be married at their age!"

With his astonishment becoming more pronounced by the second at Martha's heedless views, Phil came back, saying, "Martha, you know better than that. You're not thinking straight. What about Aunt Amy and Pa? And Lucy and Gilford Sloan were a long way from being in their teens when they tied the knot too."

"Well," Martha declared, "all that may be, but I surely don't expect to get a second go at the marriage game, and especially when I stop to consider how frisky and young-minded Bruce is and acts! Even though he is getting along in years, he still manages to do most anything he sets his mind on, bless his heart!" And, mouthing all that, Martha became hilarious with the giggles, causing Bessie, who had her arms full of table linens and was towing along at Martha's heels, to let her glee erupt once more as well.

However, neither Phil Carson nor Eliza saw any mirth in Martha's declaration.

All the same, catching Eliza's gaze and exchanging a concerned look with her before turning back to Martha, Phil said, as he studied the latter more closely, "I agree with you, Martha, Bruce does appear to be holding his own. Still, I should think that fact alone would keep the question of your marrying again from entering your head."

"Oh, come now," Martha flared back, her giggles done with on the instant. "Don't try that holier than thou stuff with me. Besides, have you forgotten that I could get divorced? There is such a thing you know!"

"Heavens! Martha!" exclaimed Eliza, wondering where the conversation was going to head to if it wasn't stopped. Are you feeling alright?"

"Certainly, I'm feeling alright, a great deal better than you are I suspect, if that drawn expression of yours tells me anything," sniffed Martha, as she drew her spine up as straight as a pine tree.

Seeing on the spot that she needed no more evidence than Martha's endeavor to get a better hold on her bearing to know that the latter had had more than one nip of bourbon that morning, Eliza knew she had to do something before the situation got out of hand. She thought the best solution was to keep a tighter rein on Martha. In brief, not let Martha get out of her sight for the rest of the day if it were possible.

Thus, laying a gentle hand on Martha's arm, Eliza said, "Martha, let Bessie finish placing the table linens. You've already done more than you should have. Run and get your coat and ride to church with Phil and me instead of coming later with the others."

Having spent the greater part of her life in the household at

Green Sea, Eliza's suggestion to Martha was not lost on Bessie. Promptly, Bessie interjected, "Yessum, Miss Martha, like Miss Eliza says, I can do that."

"No!" Martha snarled. "But when you see Bruce, Eliza, you tell him I'm seeing to everything and doing just fine."

Incredulous, Eliza said, "You've decided to not come to church today?"

"I didn't say that," Martha flared again, and with a voice that started to crack every few words, she went on, "Don't you fret – I'll be there. I won't let you down – like I'm going to be let down the next time I come to Green Sea – and not find you here. As long as I can remember – you've always been here – always – I'll never be able to stand it, Eliza – never – never." And like a sudden bolt of thunder, Martha's wails vibrated through the entire house!

Instantly, throwing both arms around Martha's heaving shoulders, Eliza soothed, "But, Martha, dear, I won't be that far away from Oak Grove, and we can visit like always. In fact, I wouldn't be too surprised to find that we'll be even closer in distance to one another."

Abruptly pulling away from Eliza's arms, Martha sobbed, "Oh, no – we won't – you wait and see. Bill Clarendon – will probably take you clear to the continent of Africa on your honeymoon – he certainly has the money – and that will take at least a year – have you thought of that?"

"No, Martha, you're upset over nothing, because Bill has not said one word to me about our going anyplace on a honeymoon," informed Eliza.

"He hasn't? Well, that's "one for the birds." declared Martha, and swiftly reaching over to the bundle of linens in Bessie's arms, she drew forth a dinner napkin and as nonchalantly as you please, she blew her nose in it and wiped the tears from her eyes.

And this inelegant move on Martha's part was the ultimate for Phil Carson, "Eliza," he said, "time is running short, and I promised Bill that I'd have you to church a little early so we must get a move on. That is, if you and Bill don't want to be caught interrupting Marsh Reed's morning worship searching for one another throughout the church when it's time to say your marriage vows."

"Yes, we must get started." agreed Eliza, as she softly and somewhat anxiously, too, let her hand rest on Martha's arm once more and added, "You will be alright, Martha, and come on to the church with the others, won't you?"

"Like I promised, I'll be there with bells on," sang Martha, her voice riding on a merry note again. Then without another word to Eliza or Phil, she whirled around and with Bessie almost in a run to keep pace with her, she bolted down the hall toward the dining room.

Overhearing Martha ask Bessie if there were any mint or parsley leaves in the pantry, Phil said, as he and Eliza made for the front door, "I'm afraid mint or parsley leaves won't be the only thing she'll be in need of if Aunt Amy gets a whiff of what's going on with her. Poor Bruce, he'll be on pins and needles all day wondering what she's going to say or do next."

"Bruce won't be the only one," Eliza said, as Phil opened the door and she stepped through it.

And so, because of the posing question of whether her cousin Martha was going to create a breach of etiquette that day, or worse still become roaring drunk, Eliza was more able to let her thoughts stray from the tremendous step she was taking than had the situation been otherwise with no bourbon indulgence on Martha's part. For what Eliza had foreseen – and it was the same for Bruce Randolph – her anxiousness over Martha's drinking was to be her primary concern for the remainder of that day's festivities. Not until it was time for her to take her leave of Green Sea was Eliza able to let her attention turn away from Martha. For aside from the time Martha Randolph was traveling to and from church and the time she spent at church that day, she continued to nip the bottle! And naturally, being aware of Martha's periodical trips to the pantry made Eliza more nervous than ever. In addition, for Eliza, what made the situation even worse was Martha stuffing her mouth full of herb leaves on every trip she made to the pantry to disguise the aroma of her drinking from others, which, of course, the herbs did not, and which caused her cousin to hardly be able to talk when she had a mind to!

Be that as it may; however, since Martha Randolph was able to keep nipping her bourbon and carrying through with the part of hostess that she had saddled herself with without falling on her face, not to mention she had never become lost to what was taking place around her as well as to what she was saying and doing, she had seen no reason whatever to not celebrate the occasion as she saw fit. For to Martha's way of thinking, she indeed had something to celebrate and in the merriest way possible. In truth, despite Martha's deep love for Eliza, Martha felt no less liberated than had she been a fish who had found its way out of a fish net. Because for more than two long years, Martha had endured and suffered along with Eliza through the latter's grief for the deceased Luke. It seemed to Martha that Eliza was forever in tears, forever telling her how lonely it was without Luke's company and never failing to add, too, how lucky she herself was to still have Bruce. In fact, Eliza had stressed to Martha how lucky she was to still have Bruce so many times that Martha had begun to be hesitant to mention Bruce's name in Eliza's presence. What's more, although Martha strived and did overlook her cousin's seemingly melancholy, it did nettle her somewhat that Eliza had never seemed to understand that she and Bruce had grieved buckets of tears for Luke, too, and still missed him terribly.

So, little wonder it was that Martha had been overjoyed to learn that Bill Clarendon had emerged upon the scene again with her joy soaring to the full. And when the couple's wedding day finally came to be, it was less wonder that Martha Randolph could hardly be expected to contain herself in a state of total temperance, to say the least.

The one and only thing that did throw a shadow on the occasion, for Martha, was when the time came for Eliza to take her departure from Green Sea. For, as Martha had sobbed this one distress to Eliza earlier, she not only saw an era ending for all time, but her future visits to Green Sea changed forever as well. But, even so, Martha had not become so befuddled with drink that she was unable to see herself making the adjustment. And, in addition, as Martha stood beside Bruce and along with the other wedding guests also on the porch at Green Sea waving Eliza and Bill off down the drive, she was also telling herself that instead of letting Eliza and Bill see her face all screwed up with tears, she was going to see them off with one of her widest smiles.

However, if her Cousin Martha was close enough to observe, the new bride, Eliza Heyward Clarendon was not returning Martha's smile. All trace of cheer that Eliza had managed to wear on her face since the beginning of the wedding ceremony and the festivities following it had vanished no sooner than the carriage wheels taking her away from Green Sea had started turning over. Now that there was no Martha around to center her attention on, wondering what Martha was going to blurt out next, or possibly tottering off her feet to the floor, the same misgivings, which had hammered at her earlier and which she thought she had conquered had jumped her all over again.

Of course, besides letting her attention center on Martha the majority of time that day, there had been something else that Eliza had learned that morning as she and Phil had traveled toward church that had helped shift her thoughts away from herself a great deal. With the carriage continuing to roll on and closing the gap between Green Sea and the Baptist church and Phil and Eliza were chattering at an easy and tireless pace with one another as they both were prone to do, Phil up and said – adding some personal philosophy as well as other news – "I've come to look at time, Eliza, as being nothing but change. To me, the two are one and the same, because as time rolls on, one can be certain that change is going to roll right along with it. Not one single thing on this earth is going to remain at its present state. No one person. No one animal or insect. No one material thing or situation is ever going to escape time's constant grind of change whether it's for the good or bad. And further, in my book, if one truly makes anything meaningful of their existence here. One must accept these alternations that do come and adjust to them and move on, or at least do their best to."

"I've loved two women in my lifetime, Caroline and Rachelle. Both were as different as day is from night. No matter though, I loved both of them as deeply as woman can know love. Now I find myself in love with still another, whose fine qualities and lovely features are all her own with no similarity whatever to those other two." He finally paused in his long say and, turning his head to Eliza, he went on and added, with a wide smile, "I gather you're not any more surprised at this disclosure than I am at finally confessing to it."

"No," Eliza smiled back. "Not really. But I do assume that the lady in question is Elizabeth Drakston."

"Yes, and I do plan to marry her, Eliza, right away," he declared and gave his attention back to his driving.

"Oh, that's wonderful news, Phil," Eliza exclaimed. "I'm so happy for you both." Then with a laugh, she went on to say, "But I am curious though, is Elizabeth on to your intentions?"

"Oh, I'm certain she is. I just haven't bent to custom and gotten down on my knees yet, that's all." He laughed back. "No, seriously," he added, growing more sober, "I'm not concerned about that part, because Elizabeth and I both already know our feelings for one another are mutual, so to me that's the important thing in any relationship."

Yes, Eliza was thinking, and in your way of trying to help me overcome the anxieties that you're aware I'm troubled with on this day, you've chosen to let me in on your feelings for Elizabeth and your plans to marry her in order to let me see that despite all the sorrow that might befall one that it is possible to triumph over it and move on with one's life.

And so, with a measure of Phil Carson's philosophy having made its impact on Eliza as well as his exciting news about marrying again still ringing in her head like Christmas bells, Eliza was able to let Bill Clarendon see a smile on her face instead of gloom as he met Phil's carriage to escort her inside the church and on down the church aisle to their designated pew. Of course, needless to say, another factor that helped, considerably, for Eliza to smile and keep it pretty much intact up until her leave-taking of Green Sea was the extraordinarily handsome and noble-looking man who was gracing her side, which in that respect is simply feminine vanity with Eliza being no different than any other woman who should happen to find themselves in the same situation! Indeed, it is doubtful there were few women in the Baptist church who were not envying Eliza Heyward on this day and for good reason at that. For not only had Eliza captured the love and security of a rich bachelor, but one whose knightly looks quickly sent a flutter through a number of female hearts no sooner than the couple entered the church. As a matter of fact, when Bill Clarendon had greeted Eliza that morning and had spared no words in telling her how lovely she looked, Eliza might have mouthed a little praise upon him too. For, certainly, Bill Clarendon deserved to hear any amount of praise she was willing to spare him!

Still slender and tall of body and sporting an ash-gray top hat in felted wool, the color the same as his fine cutaway coat and pin-striped trousers with a gray silk cravat flowing over his white silk shirt, Bill Clarendon looked every inch a king. Granted, for a couple beginning to count their fifties, Bill and Eliza both warranted all the gasps that their looks induced and showered upon them on this day.

In all events, everything had gone like clockwork all day. The ceremony itself, though short and solemn and officiated by the Reverend Marsh Reed, went off without a hitch. And following the ceremony the congregation had filed by the couple to offer their congratulations and best wishes, with a large number of these well-wishers who were family members and close friends going on to Green Sea to partake of the wedding feast in celebration of the marriage.

Ironical as it was, this was the first social function staged at Green Sea since Luke Heyward's death. All the same, if anyone were thinking about Eliza keeping to her seclusion behind the doors at Green Sea for two long years and never once opening those doors to any social affair until she threw them open in celebration of her second marriage, they kept their silence and stopped at venturing once to speculate about this unusual particular. Still, Eliza's own elderly Aunt Amy Drakston Carson came about as near to reminding Eliza about this unique circumstance, which in the new bride's view was not the best of good form, without coming right out and saying so in plain English than anyone else there.

Seated in her place of honor at the head of the long dining table, with Eliza gracing the table to her right and Bill Clarendon seated to her left facing his bride across the table, Amy Carson said, giving Eliza one of her sweetest smiles, "My dear Eliza, it does appear that through your marriage to Bill today that Green Sea has come alive once again." Then letting her gaze travel down the table to where her daughter Martha was seated and also was roaring with laughter, Amy went on to add, "Martha's almost in raptures. I truly don't think I've seen her this happy since her own wedding day to Bruce. Still, I don't suppose there's nothing like a wedding for one to get carried away. Such a happy time it is. I haven't seen so many cheerful faces for a good long while."

And, so many faces missing too, Amy Carson was thinking, but she never let on. In truth, all at once, Amy's mind was becoming so crowded with the late Matthew Carson's face, not to mention all those other faces that were absent, that she began an all-out effort to stay with the present before someone did detect the sudden pain of loss threatening to overwhelm her.

"Martha's just young at heart, Aunt Amy," Eliza said. "I don't know what I'd ever do, or would have done in these past years without her."

Matt Heyward, still captivated by all the attention Bill Clarendon had and was showering upon him and feeling his oats besides, because he had had his way with Eliza as usual, and was seated by the groom instead of eating with the twins Frankie and Lizzie off in a more obscured place, suddenly piped, "But, Grandmother, you don't need Aunt Martha anymore. You have Mr. Clarendon now! Besides, Aunt Martha is always giggling about something anyway."

Though Bill wanted to laugh and openly applaud Matt's remarks, he suppressed the urge and only let his pleasant expression remain as Eliza, under her breath, exclaimed, "Matt!" Then placing her forefinger over her mouth, she shook her head from side to side, hoping to quiet Matt before he said something far more shocking than airing his dislike for Martha's giggles.

However, far from being daunted by Eliza's sign to seal his lips, Matt, turning his attention to Bill, said, "Oh, I forgot, now that you and Grandmother are married, Mr. Clarendon, what am I supposed to call you, Step-Grandfather?"

With his kindly expression growing into a good-natured grin, Bill laughed, "No, Matt, you don't have to change one thing when you address me. You may continue to call me Mr. Clarendon, or if you like, you could call me Uncle Bill." He looked across the table at Eliza and added, "Whichever one you and your grandmother have a preference for."

No way did Bill Clarendon want to intrude upon Matt's memories of Luke Heyward, playing the role of being grandfather to Matt.

"Oh, I'd like to call you Uncle Bill. May I do that, Grandmother? Mr. Clarendon is too long to say anyhow." sang Matt.

"Of course, you may." Smiled Eliza. "And if Frankie and Lizzie would like, they may call Mr. Clarendon Uncle Bill too." She added and shifted her smile to Bill across the table and let it hang upon him for a rather long moment.

"Oh, boy howdy!" Matt gleamed, "Wait till the twins hear that! We've all got ourselves a new uncle."

"How sweet," murmured Amy Drakston Carson as Eliza and Bill continued to hold their smile on one another across the table.

At all events, although Eliza adored the Drakston twins and took much delight in every minute she spent in Frankie and Lizzie's company, her relationship with the latter was not the cozy and close relationship she enjoyed with Matt Heyward. It was simple enough to explain. Whereas Matt lived at Green

Sea and was seldom outside of calling distance to Eliza, the twins resided at Drakston Hall some distance away, which resulted into both Eliza and the twins considering it a streak of good fortune if they saw one another as often as once a week. The average was more like every two weeks or maybe a little less.

However, if Matt Heyward mostly rode herd on Eliza's heart without let-up, the same applied to Frankie and Lizzie in regard to their relationship with the older family members at Drakston Hall, and this was certainly the case relative to Amy Drakston Carson and Elizabeth Drakston. Both women near worshipped Frankie and Lizzie, not only looking on these children as a divine gift from God, but the salvation of Drakston Hall as well. To these two women, the birth of Frankie and Lizzie, with the lively sounds of their presence as well as their footsteps vibrating throughout the rooms and passageways of Drakston Hall, was truly the one marvel that had swept away the family's calamities and lifted the dark of Drakston Hall's atmosphere to sunlight again. In addition, it was most heartwarming and especially to Frank Drakston's widow to witness the happiness that seemed to hug the marriage of Frankie and Lizzie's parents, Stuart and Jane Anne Drakston. Even though time had added several years to the new of their marriage, it appeared the measure of those years had not dimmed the novelty of their union none whatsoever for either Stuart or Jane Anne. And yet, despite their enduring affection for one another as well as the obvious stability of their marriage, Jane Anne had given Stuart no more children. All the same, if this poor rate of fertility on Jane Anne's part caused Stuart Drakston to view his marriage with any less expectation than had Frankie and Lizzie had several more siblings by this late date, he did a remarkable job of hiding it!

Now as Eliza shifted her gaze away from Bill and let it travel down the length of the overlarge dining table among her other wedding guests, she could not help letting it stop and linger upon Stuart, taking note of how his eyes were making a constant play in straying back to Jane Anne regardless of who had his attention at the moment. In fact, considering how he had one arm draped across Jane Anne's shoulder even at the table – though she did give Stuart credit for the fact that both he and Jane Anne were finished eating as likewise to several others – she was thinking that if one did not know better that they would have sworn that Stuart and Jane Anne were the newlyweds instead of Bill and herself. And, such being the case, Eliza found herself regretting more than ever the bitterness she had harbored for so long against Stuart, but took heart as well that she had used her good sense and finally come through before more harm and unhappiness had come to the entire family. But, even so, and she was resolved to not give in to the urge, she would have to admit that Stuart's handsome features had a way still to stir too many long-ago memories of his late father in her mind and heart and told herself, on the spot, to concentrate on the other guests before her resolve was defeated altogether, and especially on this day.

And so, Eliza was to note besides Stuart and Jane Anne there were several more members of the younger set in attendance. For instance, Doctor Cyrus Vance and his wife, the former Grace Cooper. Bill Cooper and his wife, Harriette, sister of Doctor Vance. Yes, both children of Mollie and Brent Cooper had married into the Vance family of Foxwood Plantation in Mississippi. In addition, there were Doctor Seth Roalf Junior and his wife, Maggie, and, of course, Carr and Beth Anne Heyward, Matt's parents. Naturally, and much to Martha Randolph's ire, Laura Randolph Silverspoon and her husband, Cornwallis Silverspoon, the stage actor, were absent due to the latter's theatre engagement in Paris, France. In respect to Laura's absence, Eliza could sympathize with Martha, because Laura, her husband and their little son, Randolph, had paid only one visit to Oak Grove since Laura had married the Shakespearean actor. Also, as expected, Whit Carson was absent as well, due to being on sea duty on the high seas someplace. In addition, although Tom Green and his family continued to keep in touch with Eliza, no one in the Green family was present. But, even so, the absence of these long-time friends of Luke's caused a quake of pain to run through Eliza as she wondered when she would see them again, if ever.

All the same, as Eliza continued to let her gaze travel on, she observed that other long-time friends had come. Mollie and Brent Cooper, as well as Gilford and Lucy Sloan, the Sloan's having traveled all the distance from Lexington, Virginia; and, to be sure, the latter's obvious devotion for one another was not lost on Eliza! Still, the surprise of the day, the recluse spinster, Charlotte Clarendon, had decided to break with her staying seclusion and honor the newlyweds with her presence, which, of course, gave notice to everybody that she did approve of her brother's marriage and which, to Eliza's amusement, the Reverend Marsh Reed obviously was seeing as a golden opportunity to get into Charlotte's favor and possibly pay court to her! Noting how the Reverend was prattling away with Charlotte and the latter doing nothing but merely giving a silent nod now and then, Eliza concluded that Marsh Reed was wasting his time and would be better off to shift his attention elsewhere!

However, by the same token, Eliza was to take in how close Philippe Carson and Elizabeth Drakston had their heads nearly glued together, giving every appearance that they had become lost to all and everything around them save their interest in one another. Eliza silently rejoiced for both of them though and let her eyes move on to study another guest, the long-standing family friend and Doctor Seth Roalf Senior. Giving the doctor her eye and studying him with an intense scrutiny, Eliza decided that he had become totally resigned to all and every change that the winds of time had blown, or may yet blow his way, and found herself mentally praying that she may gain the same strength of mind someday, to hold fast to the present and its reality without letting the past slip in again and again to shake her peace of mind so violently at times. And yet, as Eliza was praying for this blessing to not look back so often, she found her mind's eye taking on the image of her long-departed friend, Caroline Wilton Roalf, as well as many other faces that might have been there but were gone from the group too, her parents, Anne and Matthew Carson, Nat, Luke, Rachelle Fillmore, Franklin Drakston, and, yes, Frank too, gone forever.

And as the knowledge of all those departed loved ones and friends came swarming in upon her like a swarm of stinging honeybees, pricking her heart and threatening to wipe out what little happiness she had managed to gain on this day, it suddenly hit Eliza that Matt Heyward was plying Bill Clarendon with far too many questions and she had best intervene instead of mourning what was past and gone and was no more.

All the same, Eliza knew she was too late to put a stop to Matt's questions, because he was already saying, "Uncle Bill, what's a honeymoon? Can you take honey from it like you can a beehive?"

Astounded, all Eliza could do at the moment was gape at Matt. She felt as though someone had slammed a board into her stomach and taken her breath away to boot. Amy Carson appeared to be no better off. Both women wanted to slide under the table out of sight. And, in the tense and heavy silence, Bill Clarendon was wondering if he could muster the courage to respond to Matt's question let alone come up with any fitting reply. Still, he knew he had to try because the question had been put to him and him alone.

So, while Matt waited, his gaze planted on Bill in earnest, the latter said, endeavoring to hold to a calm that he felt was beyond his reach by a hundred miles, "My boy, a honeymoon is a trip that newlyweds like your grandmother and myself take to sightsee different places of interest together, and become better acquainted with one another before starting their married life together." He ignored the part about the honey and was praying that Matt would not inquire into it any further.

Thankfully, Matt let the question of honey and beehives go but went farther relative to a honeymoon, asking Bill, "But, don't you know who Grandmother is yet? You sure have been courting her enough by this time to know who she is!"

Finally finding her breath, Eliza snapped, her irritation with

Matt plainly showing in the tone of her voice, "For heaven's sakes, Matthew! You know perfectly well that Bill and I know one another! And besides, you're asking him too many senseless questions!" She made an effort to tone down her voice somewhat, adding, "Listen, since you're through eating your dinner, you run on and find Frankie and Lizzie and keep them company for a while. When it's time for them to return to Drakston Hall this evening, you'll be sorry you didn't spend more time with them. Run on now and find your cousins."

Fully aware that he had surely riled his grandmother, or the name "Matthew" would not have popped out of her mouth, Matt slowly folded his dinner napkin and put it beside his plate, wondering all the while what he had said that had upset his grandmother so much that she was banishing him from the table and, on top of that, he was going to have to keep company with the twins when he knew for a fact they did not care if he was in their company or not! For all Frankie and Lizzie seemed to care about was each other and what the other was doing! He had rather talk with Uncle Bill, Grandmother or Grandpop Phil any time than visit with Frankie and Lizzie, even when Grandmother was mad with him! But maybe this time the twins might be a little help to him, help him figure out why he had made Grandmother so mad she had called him "Matthew" instead of Matt. Yes, he would tell Frankie and Lizzie all about it.

However, upon rising from his chair to carry through with his grandmother's bidding, Matt still seemed reluctant to leave as well as wanting to say something. Presently, he murmured, looking at Eliza with a most somber gaze, "Grandmother, you won't leave before telling me goodbye, will you?"

Eliza's heart gave a leap and lodged in her throat.

Making every effort to speak with a steady voice, Eliza managed to murmur back, No, darling, I promise I won't leave before telling you bye."

"Oh, goody," sang Matt, and dashing around the table he threw both arms around Eliza and was off like a shot.

"How sweet," murmured Amy Carson for the second time.

Yes, more than sweet, Eliza was thinking. This precious grandson had truly been her redemption from losing herself to the dark of grief, the one anchor she was positive that had kept her from drifting to total indifference toward life. Matt's mere presence had forced her to hold to the real world instead of dwelling in the past and becoming lost in it. Her mind had become so filled with other things today that she had given no thought to how hard it was going to be to part from Matt. Would she be able to carry it off without breaking down? If Matt cried, would she be able to bear his tears? So much still left to consider and she thought she had already covered everything.

Sensing the obvious turmoil that had jumped Eliza since Matt had left the table, Bill Clarendon reached across the table and folded his hand over one of hers in a tender, steadfast grip, which instantly brought her back from the brink of gathering tears and which she gripped his back in deep warmth. For it felt good to know that a loving, strong, man-size hand was at her disposal once again, and she was mentally praying that its strength would see her through her imminent leave-taking of Green Sea.

However, no sooner than Eliza's bridegroom had assisted her in boarding his coach for their departure from Green Sea, she was certain that her mental prayer for courage had never gotten beyond the ceiling of the dining room, if indeed it had gotten that far!

It made no difference that Matt had held his tears and she had managed to hold hers. It made no difference that Martha had not succumbed to wails of sorrow and cried out her loss as she and Martha had embraced and the latter had whispered, "Be happy, Eliza." It mattered not that Bill still held onto her hand in a loving grip. Nothing mattered and was of any consequence any more save the hard rocks that were lodged in her throat, rocks that she was doing her best to dislodge lest they cause her to suffer a total blackout and turn what had been an ordinary wedding ceremony and celebration into an alarming calamity! And, momentarily, with the happy sounds of well-wishing and cheering still drifting from the front veranda and wafting inside the carriage as it began to move down the drive, Eliza, in spite of the rocks in her throat as well as her fear of falling into a blackout, felt compelled to turn her head and look back. Though she made certain not to focus her eyes on Matt waving his small hand for all his might along with a wide grin. Instead, Eliza centered her gaze on Phil Carson and Elizabeth Drakston, taking in how Phil had one arm draped around Elizabeth's waist while he waved goodbye with the other.

Bill had turned his head and was waving also. Though as likewise to Eliza his waving could have been a little more zestful and less hesitating. Indeed, with only a heavy silence prevailing inside the carriage since the driver had closed the door upon the newlyweds, Bill Clarendon – for all the distress the thought inflicted upon his person – was beginning to wonder if his insisting that Eliza accept his marriage proposal had not been an unwise move on his part. For despite his deep love for her and even if he did sympathize with her obvious anguish over their leave-taking, Bill was too mature and level-headed to want a grieving wife whose heart yearned to be with loved ones at Green Sea, not to mention the way of life she had known there. Further, on top of everything else, Bill suddenly felt as though Luke Heyward's ghost had leaped inside the carriage and settled itself between him and Eliza. Then, just as quickly he felt chagrined for taking on such an outlandish feeling, telling himself that he had no cause to let his mind overplay on his emotions like that. The fact was, he had respected and admired Luke Heyward far too much to be thinking in terms of Luke's ghost invading any area it did not belong in.

And yet, after all was said and done, not to mention the long years in between, Bill Clarendon was not so sure that he had, at last, won Eliza. For, to him, she was giving every impression that she was leaving all and everything in the entire world that was of any importance to her, and he yearned to reassure her that that was not the case at all. He wanted to tell her that there was no cause for her to feel so downcast and by marrying him that her life was not changing all that much. Certainly, she need not feel that she was turning her back on her family for all time. But, as much as he wanted to say all this to her, for the life of him he was unable to say one word that he was positive that would fall as flat as the ground they were traveling over and doubtless sound so hollow that all sincerity in his say would be lost on her.

He could not help wondering if Eliza were thinking about Luke Heyward, possibly comparing her and Luke's wedding with the wedding that she had shared with himself today. Well, he thought to himself, if that were the case, in all honesty he could not hold her having such thinking as that in her mind against her. The truth was, from the moment he had made Luke Heyward's acquaintance, he had seen and ever understood why Eliza had fallen for the former and married him. For not only had Luke Heyward's bearing and good looks ranged above the average of men, but his impeccable manners and character were always without question to his family and fellow man as well. Therefore, the pain of losing out to a rival with such high qualities had not cut as deeply had the situation been otherwise. For instance, someone like the late Frank Drakston who had no personality traits to respect or admire. In brief, he had accepted Eliza's choice for a husband and had come to live with it. Still, had her choice been the late Frank Drakston, accepting that fact he was certain that he never would have – not in a million years!

Of course, Eliza's mind had turned back to that long ago wedding day that she had shared with Luke, but not nearly as often as anybody, including Bill Clarendon, would ever have guessed. Indeed, the wedding vows that she had repeated with Bill on this day as well as the wedding celebration that had followed afterwards and the leave-taking of Green Sea itself had so mentally and physically taxed her that she was beginning to wonder if her resolve not to break down in sobs was going to hold much longer. Moreover, when it came to comparing her wedding to Luke to the wedding she had shared with Bill on this day, to her way of thinking there was not enough similarity between the two to even consider weighing one against the other. The contrast was simply too vast and would have cast her down more than ever had she attempted it.

Yes, with not one glimmer of a cloud threatening one hope, joy or expectation that had been hers to come by, Eliza had married the man of her choice and with the approval of her father, Matthew Carson, to boot. In addition, she had married Luke a few short months following her eighteenth birthday – married him in flowing virginal white and in all the innocence and security of that young age, not to mention that bloom of youth that one has only once to bask in in a lifetime. Granted, on this day she was no longer young in age. The fact was, she was well beyond the beginning of the second half of her life so the law of nature claimed. Furthermore, considering the birthdays she had already counted and in those years had become a mother, a grandmother, and sadly a widow of more than two years standing, not only would she dare to fill her head with all the expectations she had harbored so readily in her youth, but merely hold to hope that she and Bill would have a degree of joyful experiences together to add to all the other joys in life they had already been granted.

She had lived in luxury and security. She had also dwelled on next to nothing in cash money and had made do with very little in material things to make do with for a great many years. She had labored day and night at hard work, buckling down to every drudgery in order to hold on to Green Sea and keep the wolf from the door, so to speak. She had suffered numerous disappointments and had survived the worst kind of grief. She had also endured pain and intense heartache as well. And yet, she had come into a great many blessings in life, in that, she felt she had experienced every joy and elation that love of family, love of children as well as the love of a husband could possibly bring to one.

Now she was embarking upon a second marriage and wondering with every turn of the carriage wheels that brought her closer and closer to the place she was supposed to call home, if her decision to marry again would prove out to be a mistake in the long run. To tell the truth, ever since Martha and Matt had raised those questions about going on a honeymoon, she had taken on the notion that, apparently for her, going on a trip someplace with Bill instead of starting their married life so close to Green Sea, might not be such a bad idea after all. She wondered why Bill had not thought of the fact that maybe strange surroundings were what they both needed. It was true, that Clarendon Plantation was not all that familiar to her. Still, the distance between it and Green Sea was not all that great either! So, to her way of thinking, Bill should have considered that one particular, if nothing else!

Certainly, the question of money was not why they were headed to Clarendon Plantation to spend their honeymoon. Because Bill Clarendon was far too wealthy and liberal-minded for money to be involved in any decision he made. Perhaps he just didn't have any desire to travel after spending that entire year in Europe. Then again, since Charlotte was accompanying Mollie and Brent home to Charleston today for an extended visit, perhaps Bill saw no point in their taking a trip some place because, aside from the house servants at Clarendon Plantation, they were going to be alone together, anyway.

All the same, the more she thought about her and Bill starting their married life so close to Green Sea, the more disappointment she was taking on. She wished she had the brazenness to tell Bill how she felt. Martha would without giving a second thought! Just tended to show that when it came to the question of intimacy there was very little between Bill and herself, if any. The fact was, no matter what the subject was, she shouldn't be reluctant to discuss it with him. In truth, now that their leave-taking was over with, and all the waving to family and friends had ceased, it appeared she and Bill both had become lost to the other, wondering whether to try to make conversation or just let the silence continue to grow between them – rather unique behavior for a newly wedded couple, to her way of thinking! Still, as for herself, maybe it was best that she held her silence and not try to talk. She had no idea why she felt that if she said one word, she would start wailing her head off. She wondered if what had tied her throat in knots was seeing Matt's small hand waving to them as hard as he could move his hand, never stopping as long as they held him in sight. To be sure, common sense told her that she should not feel as though she was headed to attend a funeral of a loved one instead of journeying to Clarendon Plantation to begin her married life with her bridegroom!

She had trusted that once she and Bill found themselves alone together that their relationship would have been close enough to generate more between them than a distant and stony silence. Certainly, she had expected a little more than what it appeared Bill was willing to demonstrate, but instead of him taking her in his arms and giving her some hope that their relationship, if void of passion, was going to be at the very least easy and comforting for both of them, he had chosen to say and do nothing!

Still, she must remember this man whom she had chosen to marry had been a bachelor all his mature years and was a far cry from the seventeen-year-old youth she had danced with and thrilled to so many years ago at Drakston Hall. In addition, her own behavior on this day had been nothing for Bill to cheer over. But, even so, she wished Bill would do something. All this aloofness was making her too nervous.

Suddenly, with Bill moving closer to Eliza's side, she not only was near startled but felt as though he was reading her mind, when he said, as he took one of her gloved hands in his, "Dear, I hope the carriage is comfortable enough and won't become too chilly for you before we reach home."

Now that Bill had broken the silence, Eliza was not so sure that the silence had been somewhat better, and especially in her case, anyway. For to her astonishment, she found that the rocks embedded in her throat were playing havoc with her effort to gather her voice to speak. But aware she should respond, she did manage to murmur, "No, it's alright."

Even though her voice was so low Bill was not certain his say would fit, but he took a chance anyway and said, "Well, maybe, but the weather seems colder to me." He released her hand and reached for a fur robe lying on the opposite seat and unfolding it tucked it around her, adding, "Here, this should help some until we reach the warmth of the house."

Still striving to keep the dam of tears, which persisted to hang in her throat and which threatened to spill over at any given moment, Eliza murmured again, and more distinctly as well, "Yes, I believe it does help. But what about yourself? Don't you feel the cold?"

"Not with you beside me," Bill smiled.

He felt exhilarated that they were exchanging a few words at last. And yet, he did wish that Eliza had returned his smile instead of looking so grim. All the same, he promptly dismissed her seeming sadness and went on to tell himself that her concern for his comfort did show that she was not insensitive to his presence. So, taking that as a positive sign, Bill decided that it was time that he started behaving more like a bridegroom, or more like a bridegroom who felt half as elated as he felt! In brief, declare his love for Eliza and let it show in a more personal manner. He had kept his feelings under wraps long enough.

Thus, snuggling up closer to his bride and drawing her closer to him with one arm while using his other arm to find one of her hands again, Bill said, "You've made me a very happy man today, Eliza, by becoming my bride. It's hard for me to realize that this day is in fact for real and not some dream that I'll wake up from. I do love you so and ever have."

However, if Eliza's bridegroom was expecting to hear some loving response from his bride after long months of his seemingly indifference relative to his devotion for her, he was greatly disappointed. For at this sudden and surprising cozy move and loving words from Bill, Eliza became so astounded and disconcerted that she found herself at a total loss to think of anything to say at the moment and was wondering why. But, having no desire to let Bill's loving words become gone before she did reply in kind, and gathering a smile on her face as well, she turned to him but got no further with her intentions. In that, on the instant of taking in Eliza's smile, Bill had seized her upturned face with both hands and was covering it and her mouth, too, with all the hungry passion that he had kept in check for long months. That is, he let his passion have free rein until it dawned on him that he might as well have been kissing an ice-laden lamppost and quick as lightning he was straightening up and staring at nothing and taking Eliza's coldness as not only rejecting his kisses but his love for her as well!

Never once did it occur to Bill that his stunning behavior had not only deeply jarred Eliza but near left her breathless to boot. The truth was, her breath felt as though it had dropped to the bottom of her stomach where it was fluttering in wild tailspins over and over – some delicious feeling that had also startled her, because she had more or less resigned herself to believe that those kinds of sensations were gone forever – having died along with Luke!

So, while Bill Clarendon was trying to hold onto his composure over the deep hurt and humiliation that threatened to swallow and do away with his sanity altogether, Eliza was searching as desperately as she had ever searched for anything in her life to come up with the right words to say to Bill. She wanted so much to let him know the feeling his kisses had stirred in her – words that would not sound so bold and indelicate but, at the same time, let him know that he had not offended her in the least. She felt that since Bill had held his feelings in check for so many long months that he deserved to know that his impassioned kisses had awakened feelings in her that made her aware that she could look forward to his love-making and their joining as one with a will that paralleled with his. Martha would certainly make him aware she was thinking. But how? When? Where? Oh, she felt so helpless!

All the same, that element of propriety ingrained in Eliza, a propriety her Cousin Martha possessed small amounts of if any, caused her to miss her chance once again to express herself verbally. For, all at once, Bill Clarendon was reaching inside the pocket of his overcoat and pulling forth a large envelope and said, as he motioned for Eliza to take it, "Here, I was going to surprise you with this after we reached the house, but I suppose now is as good a time as any to give it to you?"

Gingerly, and trying to deal with this additional surprise, Eliza reached for the envelope. But, no sooner than she had the envelope in her hands she was certain, knowing Bill's generous nature and his tendency to be exact in wrapping up all details, that he was presenting her with a land deed to the greater portion of Clarendon Plantation, if not his entire holdings!

Sorely disappointed and with every anxiety that she had undergone that day feeding her mind with more fuel, Eliza strained against the urge to explode but silently vented her feelings to herself, thinking that Bill Clarendon had taken a lot for granted, because she was not interested in his land! Nor was she interested in his money or whatever else he may own! All of his wealth was as remote from her mind right then as what phase the moon might be in! Besides, when it came to land and all the responsibility of owning it plus the hard work that every cleared acre demanded if any profit was realized from farming it, she was not so sure that she wanted to ever own another foot of land ever again! What's more, even if this marriage failed to work out, which in the way it's starting to head would not be a surprise to her, she already had enough personal wealth to sustain her for the rest of her days and had no interest in land ownership anymore. So, as it had been with her bridegroom a few moments earlier when he had jumped to a flash conclusion instead of having the logic to see that his unexpected show of passion might have startled Eliza, she was now doing no less in assuming that Bill had his mind planted on personal business matters and nothing else!

And, with her mind jumping here and there, it vaguely hit Eliza that Bill had said something to her. Turning her head toward him, she said, "Pardon me?"

"I said, aren't you going to see what's inside that envelope? He told her, as he did his best to raise a smile on his face again.

With her mind continuing to work overtime, Eliza was thinking, no she had no wish to look at his land deed, but she couldn't tell him that. Moreover, in her opinion, one's wedding day was no time to be discussing land deeds! Still, he was waiting so she supposed she might as well go ahead and take a look and be as gracious about the matter as possible. She had no wish to hurt his feelings, and especially over his land deed!

However, letting the envelope fall to her lap as she began to remove her gloves in order to take a good look at the document and show more interest in it besides, Eliza was telling herself when on the instant she saw that the envelope was no land deed and also was partly open showing the word passport on the papers inside!

Suddenly, feeling as though she had plunged headfirst into a river of cold water while her heart gave a wild somersault, Eliza looked at the papers in her hand more closely, observing she was holding a foreign passport to Europe made out in the full name of William Clarendon and his wife, Eliza Heyward Clarendon!

In all events, the impact of his surprise was not lost to Bill Clarendon if the expression on Eliza's face was telling him anything. It was an expression that could be telling him a million things or nothing at all, totally unreadable.

In the growing silence between them and while he waited and was wishing Eliza would say something – anything because he began to take on many doubts and wonder if he had not made a big blunder by not talking over the matter first with Eliza instead of wanting to surprise her.

Finally, after one or more long and drawn out silent minutes had passed and Eliza still had not uttered one sound, Bill chanced to say, "I do hope you're pleased, dear, I thought going away for a long honeymoon would be the thing to do, not only for us, but for the good of our marriage." He promptly thought that telling her more might be better and added, "We sail day after tomorrow from Charleston. It's a rather small but sleek passenger and cargo ship. Besides the dozen or more passengers, she'll be carrying a load of cotton to the textile mills in England. I know the captain of the ship well, a Mr. Grimmes. You'll like him, too, because he is most attentive to the care of his passengers as well as his ship. We'll be dropping anchor in the Bahamas for a few days. I wanted you to see the islands, especially the capital, Nassau. Of course, when we sail for home, we'll be taking a Cunard liner straight for New York." He suddenly concluded he had said enough since Eliza had not raised the first question or made one comment about anything he had told her. The fact was, he had become rather dumbfounded at Eliza's behavior and was wondering what to say or do next, less take a leap through the window of the carriage!

Be that as it may, Bill Clarendon was no more dismayed and rattled than Eliza was. She wanted to respond to Bill's remarks in the worst way and knew what she wanted to say besides. But feeling if she said one word she would lose all control and start wailing her head off and cause Bill to feel even worse than doubtless he had come to feel, because on top of all the other misgivings and anxiety she had borne that day, upon seeing the passports and observing the honor and thoughtfulness that he had shown in listing her name with the name Heyward still intact had been the ultimate upon the rocks lodged in her throat. She knew her resolve to keep them from hurling her into a wash of sobs was finished and, all at once, she let the envelope she was holding fall to her lap and dropping her head into the palms of her hands, she gave way to hard, wrenching sobs, sobbing like she was suffering the worst kind of grief while Bill became more stunned and dumbfounded by the second.

Though Bill was trying his utmost to understand why his surprise had aroused such a heart-rending reaction in Eliza, but he found himself unable to and had no idea how to deal with the situation and felt that it was all his fault besides. Still, he knew it was his place to try to do something and not just sit there and do nothing to try to comfort her in some way. So, although he wondered if Eliza would shove him aside or not, he suddenly threw his arm around her and drawing her closer to his side, he began to tell her how truly sorry he was for having brought her to such painful hurt.

However, to Bill's wonder, along with deep joy too, Eliza

did not shove his arm aside. Instead, she appeared to find comfort in their closeness. The fact was, he felt her snuggling up as closely to his side as possible as he continued to talk and apologize for having gone ahead and made plans for their honeymoon without consulting her first. And, presently, he was taken unawares again when her sobs began to quieten somewhat and she was murmuring to him in choked words, "No – no – you've – done – nothing to – be sorry for. It's – me."

Incredulous, and elated as well, Bill said, "You mean, you're pleased about our going abroad?"

Finally getting control over her weeping, Eliza said, "Yes, and I feel awful about breaking down like I have, but I just couldn't seem to help it."

Deeply relieved and cheered as well to know that his bride's weeping had been brought on by something other than a misstep on his part, it suddenly hit Bill that Eliza's trouble was more or less plain nervous exhaustion and nothing else.

Quickly, fishing in his coat pocket for his handkerchief, Bill said, "Turn your face to me, dear, and let me dry those tears. It's been a long and tiresome day for you, too long in my opinion. As soon as we get to the house, I'm going to see to it that you get the rest you need."

Eliza was struck again by Bill's thoughtful and considerate nature, and mentally feeling gratified for his devotion, she gave a final sniff against her water-logged throat and did as he had suggested.

All the same, as Bill began to gently blot away the tears on Eliza's face, she brought him to wonder if he really knew her at all even though he had known her his entire life when she suddenly said, agreeing with him and blurting a lot more too, "You're right about it being a long day. I knew hours ago that I should never have let Martha talk me into that celebration today. It would've been better for both you and me had we let Marsh Reed marry us in the church rectory and forgotten about a public ceremony. And the leave-taking was just too much for me, and especially with Matt standing there looking so solemn and waving us off. And, on top of everything else, I've worried all day long that Martha was going to become drunk and fall flat on her face!"

Bill was unable to contain his mirth. He threw back his head and roared out with that deep throaty laugh of his. Pulling Eliza closer still to his side, he said, "But you should know, dear one, by this late date that your cousin Martha Randolph is rather clever when it comes to her indulgence in the matter of strong drink. In all the long years I've known her, she's always been in control no matter how much or how long she nips. You shouldn't have worried so much about her."

"Well, had you seen and heard her this morning before Phil and I left for church, I'm not so sure that she wouldn't have given you the idea that she might lose control before the day ended. Phil really got put out with her."

"What did she do?" Bill asked, feeling as though a marvel had suddenly occurred between Eliza and himself since they were, at last, carrying on a normal conversation.

"Wailing her head off, saying you probably would take me to Africa on a honeymoon, and she wouldn't see me for a whole year, if then, while she picked up a dinner napkin and blew her nose in it." All at once giving thought to a honeymoon, Eliza added, "Martha wouldn't know about this trip to Europe, would she?"

Although the disclosure about the dinner napkin had amused Bill, he kept his mirth under wraps this time as he said, "I'm really not sure, she may since I did let Phil in on my plans to surprise you when I ran into him the other day in Charleston. I also asked him to let all the other family members know so they could be at the dock when we sail. I thought you'd like to see everybody again before we leave."

"Oh, Bill," Eliza happily came back, "although I do deplore goodbyes, I'm so glad you did." Then her happy expression turned more thoughtful and she asked, "Was that what you were telling Matt when I saw you talking to him just before we started for the carriage a while ago, that he would see us day after tomorrow?"

"I'd say you already know me pretty well, Mrs. Clarendon, even though we haven't been married a whole day yet," smiled Bill. "Yes, I did tell Matt that, and I also told him that when we embark on our second honeymoon, say in about two years from now, that he could tag along with us if he has a mind to, that visiting all those interesting places in England and Europe as well would more than suffice for a whole term of school work."

"You're so good with children, Bill, I do so wish that I was young enough to give..." Eliza let her voice trail off, coming to realize how silly she must appear to be wishing for something that was totally impossible for her.

However, plainly reading Eliza's thoughts, Bill felt it was vital that he put the matter to rest on the spot.

"But, dear, you're forgetting that one doesn't miss what one has never had," Bill said, tightening his arm around Eliza. "Besides, there's Matt for us to lavish our attention on and spoil as much as we like. But, above all else, you must remember that you, your love, and the comfort of your presence are the most important things in my life and will remain so from this day forward."

"But I'd so love to be young again just for you, Bill," Eliza came back somewhat wistfully. "The years have gone by and, to be sure, they've left their mark."

"Not on you as much as you think, dear. To my way of thinking, your face will always turn heads even if the day ever comes when your hair is as white as mine," Bill said.

Turning her face up to him, Eliza smiled, "I wasn't fishing for a compliment, Mr. Clarendon." It seemed natural to make a little pleasantry out of his remarks. Still, with his mouth so close to hers, to her astonishment she also found herself wishing that he would kiss her again! Those sweet sensations that he had stirred her to moments earlier were hard to lay aside and forget. "And, I wasn't flattering you just to make conversation either," Bill smiled back. But then, all at once, the light banter between them was forgotten. To Eliza, it seemed as though Bill was looking into her mind as clearly as a looking glass, for on the spot, he was dropping his mouth to hers and began to explore, seeking the warm response and tasting it that he had hoped to some moments earlier but had not. But, even so, in this second joining of their mouths, he demonstrated no frantic need on his part. Nor did he make one move to signify that he must know the depths of her feelings as well. He wanted to feel that he was being invited on this second time around, and to his elation he soon was granted his wish. For with an overlong tenderness that was soon to override every anxious nerve in Eliza's body, he began to kiss her, exploring and seeking the sweetness he found and which she never once hesitated in holding back from him until, all of a sudden, it came to both of them that no years might have fallen at all so intense their passion for one another had flamed. Indeed, they both felt as though the January day had turned to spring and had thrust them back to dwell in the springtime of their youth.

For Eliza, she had become nearly mystified to find that those compelling and sweet sensations that had been hers to experience so delightfully with Luke had been awakened again and were alive as ever, when she had been certain she would never experience them again even if she did accept Bill's proposal and they became husband and wife to the other in marriage. Now, she had truly become overwhelmed with delight to realize that this gift from God for man and woman to share as husband and wife was hers and Bill's to hold and treasure between them. And, for Bill Clarendon to find Eliza responding to his kisses so passionately was more than he had ever hoped for in his wildest imagination. He felt that he might have scaled the highest mountaintop so great was his relief and gratitude. Finally, taking his mouth from Eliza's, Bill said, as he looked down at her in adoration and a somewhat husky voice, "Eliza, dear, I guess this is what some dreams are made of. I do love you so."

Demurring not for one second in letting him know her feelings were likewise, Eliza, lifting a hand to caress his cheek, whispered back, "I think you must be right, my dearest, for you see I love you too, so very, very much."

And knowing she was speaking truth, Eliza's relief and

gratitude as well were no less than what Bill was experiencing. The fact was, Eliza felt like falling to her knees and whispering her thanks to God right then and there. For, from the day she met Luke Heyward until the day God had parted them it was her belief that only God had known the depths of her love for Luke. Therefore, now she felt that God in His infinite wisdom had given her the ability to see that she did have the inner strength to let Luke go and, finally, not only accept the love of this good, worthy man sitting beside her, but love again as well and be grateful for it.

No, she was not professing to understand Luke's untimely and unexpected death. Nor would she ever, she was certain. But, all the same, it was now her belief that through Bill Clarendon's love and devotion that her later years were going to be happy and fulfilling after all. Yes, she had thought these later years, which she had come to look on as being the second half harvest years in her life and which she had also come to foresee as being not much of anything but bleak and empty, were still going to turn a full and bountiful harvest in spite of the desolate and insignificant half she had been prepared to reap!

Breaking into Eliza's thoughts, Bill smiled, "I could kiss you all day and then some, Mrs. Clarendon, for mouthing such lovely words to me. I've waited a long time, you know."

"Would not all day be an awful lot of kissing?" Eliza shot back. "You must remember one does have to eat, not to mention breathe."

"Well," Bill grinned back, "in regard to the question of food, why would I want to eat when I have you to nibble on," and dipping his head back he nipped on Eliza's ear once or twice.

"Bill!" Eliza exclaimed, playfully brushing his head aside, "Behave, will you!" And yet, despite her protest, she was taking much delight from all those delicious shivers gathering under her clothes.

"Oh, alright, if you say," laughed Bill. "But I am warning you, there will be more of the same, a lot more."

He felt more confident now holding no reservations whatsoever in pointing out to her in an indirect manner that in spite of his long bachelorhood, and the frantic display of passion that he had made earlier, he did know how to make love to a woman!

Though Eliza did get his drift and digested it with pleasure, her cheeks flushed just the same.

Noting the blush on Eliza's face, Bill decided to drop the teasing and become more serious. He said, "We're going to have a good life together, Eliza, you just wait and see. You know one thing I'm going to do."

"I can't imagine," Eliza said, wondering what she was going to hear next.

"I'm going to purchase us one of those automobiles, a horseless carriage, so to speak," informed Bill, "just as quickly as some manufacturer starts to produce them for market."

Incredulous, Eliza said, "You can't be serious, Bill?"

"Well, I most certainly am," he smiled. "I've already seen one when I was abroad last year. This particular one was built by the German engineer, Karl Benz. His is powered by an electric ignition and differential gears and has a speed of about nine miles per hour. Just think, we won't have to fool with horses anymore when it comes to our source of transportation."

"I don't know, Bill. From what I've heard and read about these horseless contraptions, I think I'll stick with the horse!" Eliza said.

"But you haven't seen one or taken a ride in one as I have," Bill came back, in defense of his intention to purchase a horseless carriage.

"No, and I don't think I want to," Eliza told him. "I'd be scared to death."

"No, you won't," grinned Bill, "with me holding you." Then, replacing his grin with a more sober look, he went on, "Phil and I were discussing this same subject when I saw him in Charleston the other day. With all the experimenting going on by different engineers, one in particular, a young man in Detroit, Michigan, by the name of Henry Ford, we both think we won't have to wait but a few more years before we'll be able to purchase one."

"But, even if you and Phil were to get your hands on one of these inventions, are you and he certain you could operate it?" quizzed Eliza. "From what I gather it's going to take both eyes, both feet and hands, not to mention keeping both ears open for any unusual sounds and an awful lot of nerve too."

"Well," laughed Bill, "I hope I have the kind of nerve it's going to take to operate one. I'll tell you what, I'll try it out a few times by myself before I take you aboard, how's that?"

"I don't know Bill," Eliza said. "The only thing that I am certain of is, I don't plan to be anywhere nearby when you're practicing your driving skills." She laughed, adding, "I can just see Martha behind the wheel of one of those things. Considering the wild pace she sets the horse to, it would hardly be safe to get within five miles of her driving one!"

"I'll not dispute that," agreed Bill. "To tell you the truth, it wouldn't surprise me one bit if Bruce doesn't take a stiff nip every time Martha decides to drive herself someplace. As I was saying though, when it comes to the question of transportation, I'm positive it'll be only a few more years before Bruce and Martha and all the rest of us will be leaving the horse in the stable in favor of the automobile."

"It's hard to believe, but I suppose so," agreed Eliza, wondering if Phil had disclosed his intentions to marry again when the two had seen one another in Charleston. However, before she could make up her mind to go ahead and inquire if Phil had, Bill was saying, "It appears we're not going to be the only newlyweds in the family if my hunch about Phil's business in Charleston the other day is on target. In fact, he more or less said as much."

"So, he did tell you that he is planning to ask Elizabeth to marry him?" Eliza said, looking up at Bill with a somewhat anxious expression and wondering again what Phil might have said regarding his forthcoming second marriage as well as his third love.

"Well, he didn't come right out and say for certain, but he

was looking around for a suitable house to purchase in Charleston," Bill said.

"A house, what in heaven's name for?" Eliza exclaimed, wide-eyed in astonishment to think that Phil would consider living anyplace other than Green Sea.

"I suppose for him and Elizabeth to live in, but he didn't say that, well, not exactly," Bill said. "When he mentioned buying a house, he saw right off that he had fired my curiosity, so laughing, he up and said that he didn't plan on living in it by himself. You know Phil. He refused to say anymore even though I laughed too and asked him if the other party in question was Elizabeth."

"Well, he should have gone ahead and told you, because it's plain to everybody who happens to be in their company that they are in love with one another. Still, I wonder what prompted his decision to live in Charleston," Eliza said, feeling a little put out with Phil that he was considering leaving Green Sea and had not told her.

"I wouldn't say for certain, but my guess is that Phil and Elizabeth want a house to themselves," Bill said. "Come to think of it, having a household all to herself to oversee will be a new experience for Elizabeth Drakston since she's always shared those duties with other women. Besides, it's not as if she'll be leaving Drakston Hall with no mistress to oversee it. Your Aunt Amy and Jane Anne both will still be there." Turning to Eliza and showering her with a warm smile, he went on, "The fact is, Drakston Hall and Green Sea both are fortunate in that respect. There's Beth Anne, you know waiting to assume the duties that you vacated today at Green Sea."

"Yes, and I have no qualms that she'll manage just fine," agreed Eliza. "I'm also looking forward to the day when Whit leaves the Navy and comes back to Green Sea to settle down with some lucky young woman."

"You do dote on Whit, don't you, dear?"

"Yes, I do," confessed Eliza. "You see, not only is Whit the adopted son of my late father and Aunt Amy, he's a true-blooded Carson as well. So, it's only fair that he comes back to

Green Sea and makes his home there as likewise to Carr and Beth Anne and claim the heritage that is rightfully his."

Never before had Eliza spoken so candidly of Whit's birth.

"I gathered as much the first time I saw Whit after Mr. Carson adopted him. The likeness between him and your late brother was too distinct to take lightly," Bill said, not thrown in the least by Eliza's remarks.

"And the mother?" quizzed Eliza. "Did you know who she is?"

"Of course, I did, without giving it a second thought," averred Bill. "You see, it was the circumstances involved. I was in Lee's army too, at the time and knew about Nat's leave home and also about his desire to marry Lucy Randolph before his train left Columbia, SC, but he was unable to. I also knew about his effort to find a room to rent in Richmond so Lucy could come there and they could be married, but sadly, Nat's life ended at Yellow Tavern. Besides, all of us in our set were always on to Lucy's love for Nat. She had eyes for him and no one else."

"Yes, Lucy is Whit's mother," Eliza murmured, her voice filled with sadness. "I've always felt so badly that her and Nat's plans went the way they did."

"Well, in my book, Lucy Randolph did a noble deed," offered Bill. "She could not have paid Nat a higher honor when she let your father adopt Whit. The war did shatter so many lives and plans. But in Lucy's and Nat's case all was not lost. Their son did come by his true name and will also claim his heritage. So that's a lot to be thankful for. Still, I never think of the war that my sister, Charlotte, doesn't come to mind, ever wondering what her life would've been like had Orr Camden come home. I haven't told you, but Charlotte's also thinking about moving to Charleston. So, it looks like that you and I will, eventually, be by ourselves."

"Good Heavens!" sputtered Eliza, her voice registered with shock. "Is Charlotte getting married?"

"No, dear," laughed Bill, "not Charlotte ever, I should think."

"But just because we're married now, that's no cause for her to move out," protested Eliza.

"I know, dear, and Charlotte knows that too. But for quite a good while now, she's wanted to be closer to her social work and all those other activities that she's become involved in. Also, she and Mollie both would like to be closer in distance than they are, and especially now that both Mollie and Brent's children are married and live at home no longer. Now that we're married, I think Charlotte feels freer to follow through with purchasing that townhouse in Charleston that she's talked about for ever so long. Oh, don't fret, she'll continue to live at home and see about things until we return from abroad," assured Bill.

And the two newlyweds continued to chatter on about this and that and then Bill was saying, as he shifted his gaze and looked through the carriage window and across an open field bordering the road, "Yonder's the house, honey, we'll soon be home, and it'll be none too soon, if you ask me. For with the sun going down, this weather is certain to become colder by the minute."

Bill's say brought no response from his bride, however. Instead of coming back with some remark, which he had expected and anticipated her doing, she had not only said one word but appeared to have taken on an extreme tenseness, all of a sudden, not to mention some kind of expression that was totally outside his ability to read.

Eliza's strange behavior puzzled Bill, and to him, had suddenly put a damper on every ounce of closeness that he and Eliza had been able to gain and enjoy through all the chattering and physical contact they had engaged in. In brief, his bride had become beyond his reach once again! But, all the same, he decided to make no reference to her sudden remoteness and give the situation a chance to mend itself, if possible. Then, with the silence beginning to grow between them, he knew he must not remain silent and do nothing. He must come right out and ask her what was troubling her. For besides all the other things that had occurred and taxed him on this day, he had no wish to let more be added by allowing a note of puzzlement set the tone of his and Eliza's wedding night together.

Thus, much aware that the overlong and weary moment of silence was still growing in length and desiring to bring it to its end, Bill said, "What's wrong, dear? You appear to have become frightened at something. Won't you tell me? Maybe I can help in some way."

Clearly seeing the disturbance that her withdrawal had planted on Bill Clarendon's face, Eliza wanted to offer an explanation to him in the worst way. And yet, as she studied his face, her common sense told her not to offer one word in the way of trying to explain to him why she had become lost to him, as well as the present, so suddenly. No, she was certain there was no way of explaining her behavior and run the risk of him taking it the wrong way, possibly doing more harm to their future relationship than if she were to use a little tact and say as little as possible, and certainly say not one word relative to anything having to do with her marriage to Luke Heyward, and especially on this day. There was no way she could tell Bill Clarendon and make it come out right that of all the names of endearment Luke had showered her with, never once could she recall him having called her "honey". Thus, hearing Bill addressing her as "honey" had given her a turn and carried her mind back to where she no longer wanted it to dwell and certainly not on the day that she was marrying some other man!

Of course, the memory of Luke Heyward was still very much alive in her heart and would ever be so, locked there solidly forever, Eliza was thinking. But she also was aware that she must go forward and, indeed, she desired to do that. For although her comprehending of this second chance in life had been somewhat slow in coming to her, Bill Clarendon's devotion for her and his happiness were the all-important things to her now.

So, lifting her hand once again to caress Bill's cheek, Eliza said, "Not one single thing is wrong, love, and I'm so sorry I've given you that impression. I'm perfectly all right." Then, taking on a wide smile, she added, "In fact, you just keep on calling me "honey" and I promise you everything will be more than alright."

And as Eliza saw Bill Clarendon drop the troubled look on his face and replaced it with a smile of his own, and also felt his arm tighten her to his side once more in a firm squeeze, she knew for still another time on this day that she was indeed speaking the truth. The fact was, that keen sixth sense of hers was revealing it to her, disclosing it to her as plainly as when she shifted her gaze and saw the rays of the setting sun shining on the tall white columns of Clarendon Plantation in the distance.

Presently, in less than no time it seemed, the carriage was bounding up the long drive and stopping at the front steps. And with a fluster of excitement and exhilaration, which Eliza had thought she would never experience anymore, she quickly shifted herself forward on the seat out of Bill's arms and let her gaze focus long and hard upon the two-hundred-year-old ivy-covered brick mansion before her.

It had been so many long years since Eliza had seen the old stately mansion that it seemed as though she was seeing it for the first time. And, what's more and as strange as it was, she suddenly began to feel as if she were as familiar with its rooms and its hallways and indeed every board in it as she was with the entire whole of Green Sea's mansion, causing her to wonder if she had possibly dwelled in it, or perhaps another like it in some other life. Still, the thought did not disturb her. Instead, she felt a sudden warmth for it, a sense of being where she belonged, something like the feeling of a loved one's arms hugging her after a separation of many long years.

Bill, who had also moved to the edge of the seat and was waiting for the driver to pull the carriage steps down and open the door, said, "Well, Eliza, honey, we've finally made it. We're home."

Instantly taking her gaze from the mansion and letting her thoughts about it go, Eliza turned back and letting her eyes rest on her husband's face she, all at once, felt an overwhelming urge to throw both arms around his neck and, just as quickly as

150

the feeling struck her, she gave in to the urge, doing just that! Then, lightly letting her mouth brush Bill's, Eliza Carson Heyward Clarendon, whispered, "Yes, my dearest, we're home."

And, as Bill Clarendon pulled his bride closer to him, and they both became lost in an overlong embrace and kiss again, neither were aware that the carriage door had long been opened and the steps pulled down – with the driver waiting besides – until a gust of icy cold hit like a whip and startled them!

Hence pulling away from the other and taking note as well as that the driver was trying to keep a straight face and had doubtless been wondering when they were going to break their long kiss, Bill and Eliza both roared with laughter. And for Eliza it truly felt good to laugh again, and especially with this long-ago friend and sweetheart who now had become her husband.

Swiftly alighting from the carriage and giving Eliza his hand, they both still filled with laughter made a dash for the rounded, tall brick steps of the more than century old mansion. Bill, readily reached for the doorknob, and as the door was swinging wide, he gathered Eliza up in his arms and carried her over the threshold. And, as Eliza felt her feet hit the floor of the wide, elegant and grand hallway, it seemed no years had fallen between that long-ago night at Drakston Hall – Martha and Bruce's engagement party – and the present and she and Bill both were young again and eagerly awaiting the next waltz.

www.ingramcontent.com/pod-product-compliance
Lightning Source LLC
Chambersburg PA
CBHW072349090426
42741CB00012B/2979